Strange Tales from OHIO

Strange Tales from OHIO

TRUE STORIES OF REMARKABLE PEOPLE, PLACES, AND EVENTS IN OHIO HISTORY

Neil Zurcher

GRAY & COMPANY, PUBLISHERS
CLEVELAND

Gray & Company, Publishers
1588 E. 40th St.
Cleveland, Ohio 44103-2302
www.grayco.com

Library of Congress Cataloging-in-Publication Data
Zurcher, Neil.
Strange tales from Ohio / Neil Zurcher.
    p. cm.
Includes index.
ISBN 1-886228-94-9 (pbk.)
1. Ohio—History—Anecdotes. 2. Ohio—History, Local—
Anecdotes. 3. Ohio—Biography—Anecdotes. 4. Curiosities
and wonders—Ohio—Anecdotes. 5. Ohio—Description and
travel. I. Title.
F491.6.Z87 2005
977.1—dc22 2005009120

Printed in the United States of America

First Printing

This book is dedicated to these Ohioans
whose stories should someday also be told:

The late
Master Gunnery Sergeant Joe P. Velasquez, USMC
A warrior

The late
Jack Edgar Zagrans
Attorney-at-law and humanitarian

The late
Janos "Johnny" Tar
Chef and raconteur

Absent friends who are greatly missed.

CONTENTS

INTRODUCTION

We are all naturally seekers of wonders. We travel far to see the
majesty of old ruins, the venerable forms of the hoary mountain,
great waterfalls and galleries of art, and yet the world wonder
is all around us; the wonder of setting suns, and evening stars,
of the magic springtime, the blossoming of trees, the strange
transformation of the moth.

—Albert Pike

This book contains fifty years of memories—of places, people, animals, events, and legends. These are subjects that once stirred my
interest as a reporter but for one reason or another I never got to
fully explore. Now, after a half century of wandering, I have the time
to go back and take another look, to visit the places where legends
originated, and to pay tribute to some people who made a difference
in Ohio and in the world both in small and in large ways.

As Albert Pike wrote, "We are all naturally seekers of wonders"—
whether a small poem on the wall of a bicycle shop, an airplane flight
that made history, an Ohio boy in a strawberry patch who discovered
a comet, or perhaps good Ohio grass reaching up to the belly of a
longhorn steer.

In this book we visit some long-ago events and some things that
seem like they happened only the day before yesterday. Cruel as it may
sound, we witness the last public whipping in the state of Ohio. We
discover that the very last veteran of the American Revolution was an
Ohioan and a friend of George Washington. We watch in fascination
as an educator attempts to communicate with chimpanzees—and,
speaking of communication, we learn that Ohioan Thomas Edison's
last invention was an attempt to talk with the dead.

There is much, much more, including a painting that was sent to
jail, an island that actually floats, and a cemetery that sells visitors its
own brand of root beer.

Good or bad, big or small, remembered or forgotten, it all happened in Ohio or to Ohioans.

NORTHEAST OHIO

The Last Public Whipping in Ohio

MILLERSBURG

Worldwide attention was focused on a small community near Dayton back in 1994 when it was reported that an 18-year-old high school senior, Michael Fay, who called Kettering home, was arrested in Singapore and found guilty of acts of vandalism, including spray painting an automobile.

What set off the international uproar was the Singapore judge's verdict: the Ohio boy was to receive, in addition to a short prison sentence, six lashes with a bamboo cane.

Even President Bill Clinton got into the controversy, urging the government of Singapore to reconsider. It did, and the sentence was reduced from six lashes with the bamboo cane to only four. Fay received his caning, was eventually released, and came back home to America and massive media coverage.

That story set me to wondering how long it had been since anyone in Ohio had been publicly whipped for a crime. Turns out it was not so long ago as you might think. And it happened in one of the least likely places: a peaceful Holmes County farm community.

It was Tuesday, July 5, 1932.

Two brothers, 51-year-old Jesse Wynn and 48-year-old William Wynn, were arraigned before Holmes County common pleas judge Robert Putnam in the Millersburg, Ohio, courthouse. They were both charged with petit larceny. They had stolen a refrigerator and sold it to a Mansfield secondhand dealer for three dollars.

At the time they were arrested, they had been living in an unoccupied farmhouse that they had apparently broken into. Several unsolved robberies had occurred in the neighborhood. Neither of the men had a job or any source of income. William Wynn claimed that he had a family in Ashland, but he had not seen them in several months. His brother Jesse said he was from New York and had come to Ohio looking for work, then accidentally ran into his brother in Cleveland.

This was 1932, the height of the Great Depression, and thousands of people were out of work; it was not an uncommon sight to see men roaming the countryside.

Crime in Holmes County was on the rise. Judge Putnam was fuming over the increased caseload in his small court. He was quoted in the local paper as saying, "Holmes County is being inflicted with the crime wave prevalent throughout the country out of all proportions with its population." He added, "This condition must cease."

The Wynn brothers had the misfortune to be arrested at about the same time the judge was venting his spleen. The brothers were held in the old county jail next door to the courthouse for twenty-eight days while the grand jury met. The grand jury decided that, because both the men were penniless and charging them with grand larceny would only cost the county more money for a trial, it was better and less expensive to bring a finding of petit larceny, which could be quickly handled by the judge.

So on July 5 the Wynn brothers were brought before Judge Putnam. There they quickly made a mistake when responding to his questions. How were the conditions in the jail? How was the food? the judge asked.

"Very good," they replied.

"Perhaps they are a little too good," the judge observed. "You boys might like it in jail. You are both older men and know better than to steal."

The fact was, both of the brothers had bragged to Holmes County sheriff John "Peg" Stevens that they didn't care how long they stayed in jail, because they were better off there than on the outside.

Judge Putnam then asked the brothers how they pleaded to the charge of petit larceny. They both said "guilty."

The judge paused for a moment and then gave the brothers a real jolt as he announced his sentence.

He ordered them each to serve twenty days at hard labor in the workhouse on a strict diet of bread and water.

"And I mean hard labor," added the judge.

Onlookers said the Wynn brothers, who apparently had been counting on just serving time in a cozy jail with good food, appeared to be stunned by the sentence.

But the judge wasn't done.

"Or, you can each take twenty lashes of the whip and be escorted out of this county."

The two brothers immediately said in unison, "We'll take the stripes."

The judge repeated his offer, making sure the brothers understood the penalty. They said that they did and that they would rather be whipped than spend twenty days at hard labor with a diet of bread and water.

Then Judge Putnam directed that the following order be carried across the park to the jail and given to Sheriff Stevens:

> These prisoners have elected in open court to take 20 lashes in lieu of 20 days in jail at hard labor on bread and water: you are instructed as follows:
>
> You will proceed publicly at 4 P.M. Tuesday, July 5, 1932, in the front of the north door of the county jail to administer 20 lashes each to William Wynn and Jesse Wynn in the following manner:
> 1. Lashes to be applied with buggy whip or equivalent instrument by you;
> 2. Lashes to be applied to the back;
> 3. Prisoner to have no clothing on back except undershirt;
> 4. Lashes to be severe enough to raise welts but not to cut or bring blood—not to be unusually cruel—but yet, no "pink tea."
> 5. Prisoners to be taken by you to the edge of the county and turned loose.
> (Signed) Robert B. Putnam, Judge

By 4 P.M. word of the unusual sentence had spread around the town and over telephone wires to surrounding communities. There was a crowd of nearly three hundred people gathered in the center of town, outside the jail.

Sheriff Stevens was not happy about the job he had been ordered to do. As he went to the cellblock he told William and Jesse Wynn, "Gosh, I hate to do it."

He opened the cell door and asked which of the brothers wanted to go first. William, the younger of the two, came out of the cell grinning at the sheriff.

When they walked outside, Stevens had a deputy tie a rope around

Holmes County Sheriff John "Peg" Stevens reluctantly administered the whipping.

the bars in a nearby jail window and then, with William facing the brick wall, use the rope to draw his handcuffed arms over his head.

Both brothers had on bib overalls and white shirts but no underwear, so the sheriff elected to let them leave on their shirts.

The sheriff didn't own a whip and had to send a deputy to a nearby hardware store to purchase a buggy whip.

It was a few minutes after 4 P.M. when the deputy finally returned with the brand-new buggy whip. It was obvious to the crowd that the sheriff's heart was not in what he was about to do. He took several deep breaths and then, with a sigh, turned his back on the crowd, raised the whip, and brought it down on William Wynn's back.

When the whip arrived, there had been a few "boos" from the crowd, but now all was silent. All they could hear was the steady, slow, crack of the whip striking William Wynn and the labored breathing of the sheriff.

At the tenth lash the buggy whip suddenly broke. The sheriff continued to lay on the lashes, but on the sixteenth another section of the whip broke off, leaving only about a foot-long section in Sheriff Stevens's hand. The sheriff seemed frustrated by the broken and useless whip, but he had the judge's order to carry out. He took another deep breath and administered the final four strokes with just the butt of the whip. William Wynn had stood stoically through the first sixteen lashes, sometimes twisting his head to look at the crowd, but he was seen to wince as Sheriff Stevens laid on the last four blows. However, he seemed to quickly recover as he was cut down from the jail wall.

His shirt was not cut and there was no evidence of blood. He actually seemed to be in high spirits.

Then his older brother, Jesse, was brought out and tied up against the same jail wall. Someone had come up with a well-worn, old eight- to ten-foot "blacksnake" type of whip to replace the broken buggy whip. This was the kind of whip that could cut and do some damage to a man.

But perhaps Sheriff Stevens was physically tired from the first whipping, or maybe he was just tired of the whole idea. In any event, he followed the court's order and laid twenty lashes on Jesse Wynn's back, but none of them seemed to have any force. In fact, Jesse Wynn stood silently, showing no emotion, through the whole ordeal.

When he was released from the wall to join his brother, they were seen smiling and talking to the sheriff as he loaded them into a sheriff's car for the ride to Loudonville and the Holmes County line. There they were let out of the car and told to leave Holmes County and to not return. They were last seen walking away and waving to the sheriff.

Judge Putnam did not attend the whipping, although he could have seen it if he wanted to from his window in the courthouse, which overlooked the lawn by the county jail.

The incident released a firestorm of publicity. The story of the whipping, the first in more than fifty years in Ohio, swept the state and the nation. Judge Putnam was both hailed and criticized. A *Cleveland Press* editorial called him a "cheap tyrant of the bench" and said, "Judges who are bent on restoring the torture system for their private entertainment should be retired to private life as soon as the electorate can get at them."

But there were also those who praised the judge for trying to do something to stop the perceived coddling of thieves and burglars that was on the rise in America because of the Depression.

The judge responded to his critics by writing a letter to the local newspaper explaining his reasons behind the unusual sentence and hinting that he might do it again. He wrote, "This court is determined to do all in its power to restore this community to normal conditions and to halt crime in Holmes County." Quoting Thomas

Jefferson, he said he was "prepared to stretch all the laws until they crack" if it would help end the crime problem.

The majority of Holmes County residents apparently approved of Judge Robert B. Putnam: he served nearly thirty years on the bench, retiring in 1960 as a judge of the appeals court.

Sheriff Stevens only held office for one term. He was defeated in his attempt at reelection.

The Wynn brothers seemed to disappear after being released at the Ashland–Holmes County line

The county jail where the whipping took place is now home to the Holmes County Commissioners. The building is on the National Register of Historic Buildings. It is located at the intersection of State Routes 83 and 39 in Millersburg, Ohio.

The Eccentric Elys of Elyria

ELYRIA

The Ely family, who founded the county seat of Lorain, was, to say the least, a bit different. One of the descendants carried crutches with him every day of his life, even though he had no need for them. Another virtually imprisoned himself and his only son in a rotting mansion for more than sixty years because he couldn't get over the loss of his wife. And the wife of one Ely kept moving and hiding the body of her husband when a dispute broke out over a mausoleum for the family.

It was in 1817 that Heman Ely founded the city of Elyria. (He was also responsible for naming the county Lorain, because it reminded him of a similarly named town in France that he had once visited.)

No one can say that the Ely family has not been good to the city that bears its name. Heman donated to the new town the land on which the county courthouse would be built, as well as beautiful Ely Park in the center of downtown. Trust funds set up by the Ely family still benefit the city today.

Perhaps that is why many of the Ely family's eccentricities and their sometimes very questionable behavior have been ignored, or at least not recorded.

Take Heman's son, Albert Ely.

Albert went without stockings, instead putting fresh sawdust in his shoes each day. He would stomp down the street leaving a trail of sawdust wherever he went.

He always carried a pair of crutches, although he had no physical disability. He said he carried the crutches just to be prepared, in case anything ever happened.

He refused to be photographed. In fact, the only known picture of him in existence shows Albert Ely from the back, walking away from the photographer, carrying his crutches.

He was a college graduate in a time when few people achieved a higher education, and he was said to be a mechanical genius. He was also known for being overly concerned with being fair to everyone—to the point of eccentricity. He often paid more than the asking price for merchandise, and in court cases he actually took the stand to testify against himself, causing frustration for judge and jury as well as his attorney.

Then there was Heman Ely's grandson, Charles. Charles Ely decided to build an enormous mansion on a 1,400-acre estate that today would encompass Washington Avenue, Cascade Park, and Elywood Parks in Elyria.

However, before the mansion could be completed, Charles died at the age of 35 in a Cincinnati insane asylum. His wife, Louise, oversaw the completion of the home, which became a gathering place for the rich and famous of Lorain County and northern Ohio. She also helped establish

Albert Ely insisted on carrying crutches with him everywhere he went, "just in case."

the city's first public library and donated the land to create Elywood Park. Then tragedy struck again. At a twenty-first-birthday party for her son, William, Louise suddenly died, leaving the 21-year-old William heir to the mansion and the Ely fortune.

William Ely was a student at Ohio State University at the time and had met a pretty 20-year-old brunette coed by the name of Iovia "Kitty" Fisher. With his mother and father gone, he directed his love at Kitty. They soon married and moved into the great Ely mansion. By all accounts it was a happy marriage. They were young, wealthy, deeply in love, and popular with members of the society circles in which they moved. They had a stable of fine horses, which they would ride across the hundreds of acres of the Ely estate. The house had the best in lace curtains, imported carpets, and furniture. Life for William and Kitty Ely was very good.

And it became even better the year following their marriage when Kitty gave birth to their son, Arthur Ely. It was a joyous time for the young family. But before the year was out, the unthinkable happened. Kitty Ely developed stomach cramps and a high fever. Doctors were called to the Ely mansion, but they were unable to relieve her pain, and before the day was over Kitty Ely was dead, apparently the victim of a burst appendix.

William Ely was inconsolable. He was only 23 years old and a widower with an infant son. He sat long hours by Kitty's casket, talking to her in a low voice, promising to always love her, to never change ... never.

William Ely was so wrapped up in his bereavement, even after Kitty's funeral, that he went into seclusion, leaving the care of baby Arthur to the family's domestic staff and kindhearted neighbors.

With Kitty's death the lights and the gaiety had gone out forever in the Ely mansion. William did no entertaining. He refused visitors. He instructed his household workers to leave everything exactly as it was before his wife died.

As the days stretched into weeks and the weeks into months, and finally years, life in the Ely mansion continued, but William Ely was a changed man. He was continually sad and depressed. When friends would point out that he was only in his twenties and had time to meet someone new, to start another family, he would only smile faintly and shake his head.

Arthur Ely in his later life would recall this tragic time and write: "In my father's eyes the helpless infant was to blame for the stunning loss of Kitty. A father's love turned into bitterness and hate. Thus began a nightmare existence in which the shadows of hunger, cold, and privation surrounded us for more than a half century."

When constructed in the late 1800s, the Ely mansion was a showplace.

When a household employee decided to dust the mantle where William Ely had stopped a clock when his wife died, moving some articles and putting them in different places, William was outraged. He fired the woman on the spot. He refused to let anyone touch the clock. He had a miniature of his wife's tombstone carved and placed in his library at the mansion. The horses they had so loved to ride were sold.

William began to travel, leaving his small son in the charge of his household staff. But whatever he was seeking he did not find, and each time he returned to the gloomy mansion he seemed more morose than before.

When Arthur was a teenager, William suddenly fired all of his help, and the two of them retreated into a couple of rooms in the deteriorating mansion.

Arthur later wrote, "He ordered the last of the housekeepers from the house and never again until his death did anyone care for the house. The lace of the window curtains, once the envy of the community's housewives, faded and came apart as the curtains hung in front of the grime-encrusted windows. The rugs rotted away on the beautiful flooring and spiders made their home in the debris."

The furnace in the home stopped working, and William refused to spend the money to fix it, although he had thousands of dollars in the local banks. With no heat, the mansion deteriorated further. Plaster started falling; a hailstorm broke a window, which was not repaired. Birds and other animals found their way into the parlor, which was still, eerily, exactly as it had been when Kitty Ely died, though now draped in cobwebs and dust.

Arthur Ely said he constructed what he called an "igloo" in his bedroom by draping his bed with canvas sheeting and keeping it warm with a small kerosene heater that he managed to purchase without his father's knowledge.

Finally a family friend, concerned about the hermitlike existence of the two Elys and having been repeatedly rebuffed for suggesting that William Ely install gas heat, spent his own money to have a gas line run into the mansion.

William Ely grudgingly accepted the gift but would go into his son's room at night, even during extremely cold days, and order him to turn the gas to low. He kept the temperature at a constant 60 degrees.

For years, the only food the pair had was the cheese, oatmeal, crackers, and bologna that William would periodically go out and purchase.

The water pipes had stopped working in the old house, and father and son had to carry water for drinking and bathing from an old well on their property.

When Arthur was a young man in his twenties he met a girl, fell in love, and asked her to marry him. He went to his father to make the announcement and to plead with him to allow the prospective newlyweds to take over a small cottage behind the mansion as their home. William Ely glared at his son and stalked out of the room without saying anything.

The next morning, Arthur was awakened by the sound of pounding. Looking out the window, he saw a crew of workers tearing down the cottage. His father walked in, pointed to the half-demolished building, and said, "There is my answer."

Arthur Ely said it was just one more example of the lengths to which his father would go to make sure that he never experienced any happiness; Arthur said William would tell him, "To love is to lose. To love is to be savagely wounded and terribly hurt." He still blamed Arthur for Kitty's death.

The years had stripped the paint from the old mansion. It was now

In the 1940s the rotting, crumbling mansion still housed the grieving William Ely and his son, Arthur, whom he held as a virtual prisoner.

just a graying hulk, and to neighborhood children it was a spooky house where an old man and his son lived mysteriously.

In October 1946 William Ely finally found the peace he had been seeking since Kitty's death in 1883. With William's death, Arthur Ely was finally freed from his father's influence and control. One of his first actions was to call a wrecking company to tear down the mansion that had been his home and prison for his entire life.

He took a final walk through the dusty interior just before the demolition crew started their work. On the mantle over the fireplace, coated with decades of dust, lay a sprig of long-dead holly, placed there sixty-two years before by the mother he did not remember. He looked at it for several moments and then told the contractors to start their work. "This house," he said, "has been lived in long enough."

But the Ely saga does not end there.

When his father died Arthur Ely was already in his sixties. He used some of his inheritance to build a rambling modern stone home on a corner of the property where the old mansion once stood, and he became a familiar figure in downtown Elyria. Just the opposite of his father, he seemed to welcome friends and company. Then Arthur met Sally.

Helen Catherine "Sally" Jasany was very different from Arthur Ely.

He had been born to wealthy parents, an only child from pioneer stock. She was one of nine children born to her Cleveland parents in a family where dollars were few and far between.

Sally Jasany was by some descriptions a "tough broad," a hardworking lady who said what she thought. She was raised on Cleveland's near west side near the steel plants. Her earliest memory was carrying her father's lunch pail to him at the plant where he worked, sometimes carrying home a pail of beer that he had purchased at a nearby tavern.

By 1939 she had had two failed marriages and moved to Elyria, where she owned the Northwood Inn, a bar on Broad Street.

The Northwood was a workingman's place, and Sally knew all the regulars. But in the late 1940s one white-haired guy came in daily to order her soup. He really seemed to like the soup, but he also seemed to like *her* very much. She was surprised to learn that he was Arthur Ely, the last heir to the Ely estate.

Sally and Arthur's marriage in 1951 caused a scandal. Gossips all over the town said that Sally had married Arthur for his money. One observer, though, disputed the gossip. Don Miller, a longtime writer for the *Elyria Chronicle-Telegram*, noted that when Sally married Ely she already owned her own home and business and had over $70,000 in the bank, a sizable sum in the early 1950s—hardly the profile of a woman "marrying for money."

The most important fact was that Arthur loved Sally. He was quoted in an interview as saying, "I have found a life where there is fire in the winter, where the table is full, where I can peer from the windows and see flowers about the house. And she makes me laugh."

For the first time in his life, Arthur Ely was content.

In private he told friends that he still had nightmares about the old mansion and feared being trapped in a burning building. He made Sally promise him that when he died she would not bury him below ground. He designed a marble mausoleum intended to hold not only himself and Sally but also all the rest of his family—including those already buried in Ridgelawn Cemetery.

Arthur and Sally only had a little more than seven years together before he passed away on November 4, 1958.

But even in death the story of Arthur Ely took some strange turns.

Arthur Ely, after living fifty years in a crumbling mansion, finally found happiness when he married Sally Jasany in the later years of his life.

Sally tried to keep her word to Arthur. His embalmed body was placed in a city-owned mausoleum at Ridgelawn Cemetery, awaiting the building of the Ely Mausoleum.

But the Ely estate trustees declined to approve the $32,000 cost of the marble-and-granite memorial structure. They objected on the basis of the Ely will, which stipulated that most of the funds from the estate were to be used "for the benefit, education, enlightenment, comfort and enjoyment of the residents of the city of Elyria, Ohio." They didn't think a pink mausoleum fit that description.

For two years nothing happened. Then a man by the name of Gerald Martin roiled the waters with an interesting discovery: for two years Ely's body had been lying not in a crypt in the city-owned mausoleum, as expected, but on some sawhorses in a storage room. Martin claimed favoritism.

"They made me seal my mother in a crypt," Martin complained to the city health department. He demanded that the city force Mrs. Ely to either bury her late husband or have him sealed in a crypt. He also threatened to have his own mother's body removed from her crypt and taken to his home on Second Street and to keep her body in his living room. The city solicitor was asked to determine officially if a body had to be buried.

It was at this point that Arthur Ely's body disappeared from the receiving room at the city mausoleum. Clarence Ziemke, a cemetery official, pulled into the cemetery just as a hearse pulled out. He soon discovered that Ely's body was missing. Later that same day the local papers reported that Sally had had the body removed to a local funeral home in order to stop the city from forcing her to bury her husband.

Reporters then received a tip suggesting that Gerald Martin should be asked if it was true that he carried around in his car a steel container holding the embalmed body of a dead family dog. Reporters did just that. Martin denied it, but then under heavy questioning he admitted that the dog was no longer in his car but in a southern state that he did not identify. It turned out that the tip came from Sally Ely.

The cemetery hassle became more heated. Martin insisted that since Sally didn't have to bury Arthur, he wanted to take his mother out of her crypt and place her in the storage room where Arthur had reposed for over a year.

Sally had Arthur's body moved again, this time to another storage area, and even threatened to have all of the Ely ancestors then buried in Ridgelawn Cemetery dug up and moved to another city.

Despite the legal wrangling and the threats, Sally could not convince the Ely Trustees to fund the mausoleum Arthur designed. And when a public fundraising drive to build the mausoleum also collapsed from lack of support, she threw in the towel.

On May 29, 1962, a small private funeral service was held at Ridgelawn Cemetery. Only a handful of people were there. The pallbearers were members of the Elyria Park Board. Arthur Ely was buried next to his mother, Kitty Ely.

Asked why she finally agreed to the burial, Sally Ely said sadly, "It was so the dead can have the peace so long denied them."

The Murder of George B. Saxton
CANTON

George B. Saxton of Canton, Ohio, had it all—wealth, good looks, a prominent family, and an eye for young, good-looking ladies. Married, unmarried, it didn't seem to bother George.

He nearly married, twice. His first fiancée was a young woman from Canton described as a "socialite." But just before the big day, George got cold feet and broke off the relationship. It's said that the woman was so distraught she soon sickened and died. Many claimed a broken heart caused her death.

George Saxton had an eye for the ladies—and a problem with commitment.

The death of his former girlfriend didn't seem to faze George. It wasn't long before he was engaged to a prominent young woman from Massillon. This time the wedding day arrived, but George didn't. Reportedly, the second jilted fiancée was so upset that she later eloped with her wealthy family's chauffeur.

George, it seems, had a problem with commitment.

His next encounter was with a married woman. Her name was Annie George.

Annie and her husband, Sample George, lived in nearby Hanoverton, where Sample was a carpenter. Looking for work, Sample and Annie, along with their two children, moved to Canton.

They rented an apartment in a building known as the Saxton Block, which happened to be property owned by George Saxton.

Annie, a beautiful brunette, was shopping in a Canton store one day when George Saxton spotted her. He was so intrigued by her looks that he followed her around the store and finally managed to introduce himself to her. Discovering that she was doing some sewing and alteration work to help make money for her family, Saxton began stopping in at the George apartment with small sewing jobs.

There was an instant mutual attraction, and it wasn't long before the attraction turned into a love affair. Anna left her husband. Sample George filed suit against George Saxton for alienation of affection, but Saxton's attorneys did their best to tie up the suit in court for years.

Saxton convinced Annie that if he was to marry her, she must get a divorce from Sample. Getting the divorce in Canton would necessarily involve Saxton, and with his social position in the town that would not be a good thing. So he offered to send her to South Dakota, where after six months of residency she could quietly file for a divorce, and no one would be the wiser back in Canton, Ohio. Saxton said that he would pay all of her expenses out west and stand by her when it came time for the divorce, which would free her to legally become Mrs. George B. Saxton.

Annie had obviously not heard about George's two previous promises to marry.

She packed up and moved to South Dakota, and for the next six months George, true to his word, sent her expense money. Occasionally he would make a hurried trip to spend some passionate days and nights with her.

But when the divorce was final and she was able to come back to Canton, Ohio, Annie did not get quite the reception she expected.

George Saxton, it seems, had discovered some new friends during Annie's absence, and instead of producing the wedding ring she expected, he laughed at her. When she brought up the subject, he said he was not ready to get married. As the days went by she saw less and less of George, and it became apparent, even to her, that he was avoiding her. Now, when George had dropped women before, they had conveniently pined away after him, and one even died of a broken heart. But Annie George was a different kind of woman. Her back was against the wall. Here she was, a divorced woman with two children and no income, and now the man who had claimed to love her and had promised to marry her was attempting to dump her. She wasn't going to let him get away with it.

First she filed a breach of promise suit against George Saxton. But again his prominence and his contacts worked in his favor. After a year of legal haggling, the suit was dismissed with George denying he had ever promised to marry her.

So Annie tried another approach. She would show up in restaurants and stores where he might be meeting other women and cause a scene. Finally Saxton went to court and got a restraining order to stop her from bothering him.

But that didn't stop Annie. She repeatedly threatened Saxton and seemed to know everyone he was seeing and where they went. She also filed suit again against George, this time to regain her furniture, which was in her former apartment in Saxton's building. Annie did everything in her power to make George Saxton's life miserable.

But by this time George had a new love. A young widow by the name of Eva Althouse.

One evening when George and Eva were out for a bicycle ride, Annie, in a rage, suddenly confronted them, raising a pistol and pointing it at the pair. She ordered George to come with her to her apartment. He left Eva with the bicycles and accompanied Annie to her home, where she launched into a tirade about his failure to marry her and threatened to kill him if she ever caught him again with Eva Althouse.

Anna "Annie" George was a woman scorned, but was she capable of murder?

George was finally able to calm her and leave. However, Eva Althouse went to court and requested that Annie be placed under a peace bond and ordered to keep away from her. This was done, and the courts warned Annie to leave the couple alone.

About this time the old alienation of affection lawsuit filed by Sample George finally came up for trial. Fearing that Annie, in her wrath, might actually testify for her former husband, Saxton decided he had to do something to derail the suit, and so he set out to make amends with Annie. He asked her to testify that it was not his affection for Annie that caused the breakup of her marriage but rather Sample George's brutality and beatings that had prompted the divorce. He promised that this time he really would marry her. They even went so far as to set the date for the wedding.

As the date for the trial drew near, powerful friends of Saxton's worked behind the scenes to try to settle the matter out of court. They were successful, and George Saxton finally made a lump payment to Sample George and ended the case without it becoming a media circus.

The following day he was seen having an intense conversation with Annie George, and she told friends that she had demanded he keep his promise and immediately marry her. He apparently told her it would have to wait.

Shortly before dark on Friday, October 7, 1898, George Saxton was approaching the steps to Eva Althouse's residence when a woman dressed in black approached. If there was a conversation, no one heard it. A witness later said that from a distance he saw the woman draw a gun and shoot a man twice. The man fell to the ground, and the woman calmly started to walk away. When the man cried out in pain for help, she turned, walked back, and without any emotion shot him twice more before finally disappearing into the dusky night. George Saxton lay on the sidewalk, dead.

Saxton's family and friends had long been concerned that George's romantic shenanigans would erupt into a scandal in the media. But now, with his murder, the scandal they all feared would be not just fodder for the local media in Canton but a nationwide story. That's because Saxton, in addition to being a prominent local citizen, was also the only brother of Ida Saxton McKinley—the beloved wife of the twenty-fifth president of the United States, William McKinley. News that the brother-in-law of the president of the United States had just been gunned down, presumably by a spurned lover, would spread far and wide.

Canton police were very familiar with the threats that Annie George had made to both Saxton and Eva Althouse. They immediately went to Annie's home.

She was not there. The police began checking around the town, while staking out her home. Reports started filtering back that she had been seen in several places downtown and at one point was spotted just two blocks from Eva Althouse's home.

At about a quarter to nine that evening, Annie George came strolling up to the front door of her home. Policemen immediately arrested her. She refused to answer any questions and asked that her attorney be called.

She would not answer any questions about her whereabouts that evening or say if she knew anything about the shooting. The same was true at the jail, where the prosecutor bombarded her with questions about her threats toward Saxton, asking why she was refusing to talk. All she would say is that she wanted to speak to her attorney. She was charged later that night with the murder of George Saxton.

The McKinleys were holding a reception at the White House when the news was whispered to the president. He ordered that Mrs. McKinley not be told until after the reception, when he would be able to break the news to his wife alone. She immediately collapsed when she heard of her brother's murder and had to be carried to her room.

As the news swept Ohio and America, Annie George became something of a celebrity. Reporters tried to get in to see her in her cell at the county jail, but her attorneys were allowing no one to speak with her except old trusted friends, and there was to be no talk of any kind about the murder.

The following Monday, President and Mrs. McKinley arrived in town for her brother's funeral. Reporters from all over the country were in Canton to cover the story. But the funeral was private; only the family and a few close friends were admitted. The president made no public comment on the killing of his brother-in-law. Soon after the funeral, President and Mrs. McKinley left for a scheduled appearance in Chicago.

Annie George was eventually indicted and tried for the death of George Saxton. But in those days before DNA, fingerprints, laboratory tests, and other technical investigation methods, the county prosecutor had little to work with. No one had actually seen Annie George at the Althouse home that evening.

Doctors testified that a smudge on Annie's hand, which police claimed to be gunpowder residue, was just plain dirt. What it all boiled down to was simply a case of circumstantial evidence. Also, Annie was represented in court by one of the county's finest defense attorneys at that time, James Sterling, who painted a picture of George Saxton to the jury as a "destroyer of families," a man who never could truly call a woman "wife," and a wealthy man who had many enemies, any one of whom could have been the killer and may have used the threats that Annie George made to cover his or her tracks, knowing she would be the immediate suspect.

It took the all-male jury all night to bring in a verdict of not guilty. The murder case of George Saxton was never solved.

The Saxton home is today the National First Ladies Library and Museum.

George Saxton's brother-in-law, President William McKinley, was also murdered four years later, on September 6, 1901, while shaking hands at the Pan-American Exposition in Buffalo, New York.

His murderer, Leon Czolgosz, also from Ohio, was captured moments after the shooting. Czolgosz was quickly indicted, tried, and convicted, and less than sixty days later, on October 29, 1901, he was put to death by electrocution. Justice, though not always certain, was swift in those days.

America's First Black Politician

BROWNHELM

John Mercer Langston was born in Virginia, but he made history when he moved to Ohio.

Langston was born on a Virginia plantation. His father was Ralph Quarles, the white owner of the plantation. His mother was Lucy Langston, born a slave on the Quarles Plantation but given her freedom by her lover.

When he died, Quarles left his entire estate to Lucy Langston and her three sons, including John. The windfall enabled them to leave Virginia and move to a free state. The state was Ohio.

John Mercer Langston entered Oberlin College (the first college to open its doors not only to women on a coeducational basis but also to African Americans). A brilliant man, he received several degrees, including a master's degree in theology in 1852.

He wanted to be an attorney but was turned down by every law school he applied to because of his race.

He finally found an Elyria attorney, Philemon Bliss, who let him read law in his office (a common practice in those days for people who for one reason or another could not go to law school) and helped him pass the Ohio bar exam, making him Ohio's first African American attorney.

With some of his inheritance Langston had purchased a fifty-acre farm in the small township of Brownhelm in Lorain County. He was the only African American in the all-white farm community, but because of his education he was much sought after for his advice and counsel. In 1855, years before the Civil War, Langston was elected overwhelmingly to the post of township clerk, becoming the first black man ever elected to public office in the United States—at a time when African Americans were still being held as slaves in many of the United States—a time when even in northern states life was very difficult for anyone with black skin.

After being elected the first African American public official, John Mercer Langston wrote to a friend and said that he thought his election might signal a new day for people of color in America.

Langston would go on to an incredible career that included terms as acting president of Howard University, minister-resident to Haiti, and president of Virginia Normal College. In 1889 he was elected a representative from Virginia to the U.S. Congress. Active in Republican politics, he was so highly regarded that he was twice suggested as a candidate for vice president of the United States.

Shortly after his very first election, Langston, justifiably proud of his achievement, wrote to his friend Frederick Douglass, telling him the news and predicting that his win might mean the beginning of a new and better relationship between the races in America.

Although he spent his life working for equal rights for African Americans, he did not live to see his prediction come fully true. He died in Washington in 1897.

A memorial marker to the memory of America's first elected African American public official stands in front of the Brownhelm Community Building on North Ridge Road in Brownhelm.

The Man Who Built a City

BARBERTON

Hi Barber was not a man to be argued with. When he wanted something, he had the wealth to make sure he got it. And if wealth wasn't enough by itself, he knew how to spend money to make his point.

His full name was Ohio Columbus Barber.

That name may have been chosen because his father, a Connecticut barrel maker, had just moved to Akron in time for the birth of his son in 1841. It's believed his father was inordinately proud of his adopted home state. As for the "Columbus" moniker, most folks aren't sure if it was because it was the state's capital or because George Barber happened to admire Christopher Columbus. In any event, as the boy grew to manhood he rarely used his full name.

To his family he was Hi. As he grew older, most folks referred to him as "O.C." But whatever they called him, he became a man to be reckoned with.

George Barber had bought an Akron company that manufactured matches, and at age 16 Hi Barber was given a horse and buggy and sent off by his father to sell matches.

He must have been a good salesman, because ten years later Hi Barber went into business for himself, buying a machine from Sweden that could cut diamond-shaped matches. In a short time he was producing two million boxes of "diamond" matches each year. In that time before child labor laws, he hired many children for the dangerous work of dipping the wooden sticks in sulfur and then into phosphorous.

By 1880 Hi Barber was the manufacturer of one fourth of all matches made in the country. He sold about six billion matches in 1880. He was a very wealthy man.

Barber was putting together a business empire. He brought twenty-eight companies under the name of the Diamond Match Company. He controlled factories across the country and large forests for raw materials. He was O. C. Barber, the "Match King."

Barber decided to build the new town to consolidate his growing empire of companies and give them room to grow. So he set out to build a model town, even bringing in a noted town planner to lay out

No expense was spared in building the Anna Dean Farm—even the barns resembled fashionably built homes.

the new community.

Barber left Akron and went west to Norton Township, where he owned 550 acres of land. Here he decided to build his new city. He even named it after himself, Barberton. (He named the lake in the center of the community after his daughter, Anna.)

It was said the town grew like magic. People started calling it the Magic City.

So how do you top building a city and naming it after yourself?

Ohio Columbus Barber decided to build the greatest farm in America, and perhaps the whole world.

He would build it just outside of Barberton and call it the Anna Dean Farm, after the same daughter for whom he had already named a lake, and his son-in-law, Arthur Dean Bevan.

Barber had in mind something so large, so magnificent, that it would last long after his time on earth. He almost succeeded.

The original farm consisted of almost three thousand acres. The farm's gatehouse and coach house were small mansions. And what he called barns looked more like ornate offices; they were of French Colonial design, with turrets on the barns copied from castles in Germany. They were huge, too: Barn Number 3 was eight hundred feet long and forty feet wide. The greenhouse near the main house had over twelve acres under glass. The pig barn was christened the Pig Palace by workers. Silos were built to hold a thousand tons of feed, and their tops looked like bell towers. By the time Barber was done, his grand farm had 101 buildings.

For the imported herd of a thousand registered cattle, the barns were designed so cows would not have to walk in their own waste. A pit below the cows gathered the manure. The barns were lighted with electricity and had running water and even an air-circulating system—this in a time when many people still were using gas or kerosene to light their homes.

Barber's plan was to make the farm a model for American agriculture. He willed the entire farm to Western Reserve University with the stipulation that it be used as a place to solve agriculture problems and find better ways to farm.

But what Barber had not planned for was the number of creditors that would file liens on the property when he died in 1920. The liens totaled almost six-and-a-half-million dollars. The university decided it could not pay those bills, nor did it have the estimated one million dollars a year that it took just to operate the farm, so the property was eventually broken up and sold for development. Of the dozens of barns and outbuildings that once made up the estate, only a few remain. The Barberton Historical Society maintains three of them so that future generations can see a bit of the dream of the man who built their city.

O. C. Barber had hoped to give a gift to the future. But perhaps something he said in 1915 turned out to be prophetic: "The Anna Dean Farm can give you what you need, all that you desire, and more than you deserve."

The Barberton Historical Society, P.O. Box 666, Barberton, Ohio 44203, www.annadeanfarm.com

The Inflatable Airplane

AKRON

If Ohio is the birthplace of aviation, it doesn't seem surprising for it to have given birth to a rather, well, different kind of flying machine.

I speak of the Inflatoplane or, as the Akron-based Goodyear Tire and Rubber Company officially named it, GA-33.

It was an invention that some say was before its time, while others think it was more like reinventing the Model T flivver.

As the name "Inflatoplane" implies, it was an airplane that could be inflated, blown up like an air mattress or a swimming-pool float. The idea was to make a lightweight plane that could be used for military purposes—for example, rescuing downed fliers by dropping them a package by parachute that contained an airplane, which they could then inflate, attach a motor to, and use to fly themselves to safety.

The final product looked a lot like a giant version of those little inflatable airplanes on a stick that are sold to children at air shows and carnivals. But the Inflatoplane had a wingspan about comparable to those little two-seater yellow airplanes that everyone used to learn to fly, the J3 Piper Cub.

Deflated, the Inflatoplane could be folded into a self-contained package that looked like a large lumpy wheelbarrow. It took five minutes to inflate the aircraft, and it required less air pressure than an automobile tire. The whole thing weighed just 240 pounds and had a wingspan of 22 feet and a length of 19 feet, 7 inches. It had a two-cycle engine (think Moped or small motor scooter) that put out forty horsepower. The craft had a twenty-gallon fuel tank and was designed to carry men and equipment weighing up to 240 pounds.

Test flights of the craft were begun at Goodyear's Wing Foot Lake Facility in Akron, Ohio, in December 1955. The tests also attracted the interest of the U.S. Army, which sent pilots to Akron to be trained to fly the Inflatoplane. But while the idea was a good one, there were a few problems. According to men who test-flew the craft, the inflated wings were unstable and had a tendency to flap, and in at least two instances they hit the propeller, which tore a hole in the wing, letting the air out. In one case the pilot was able to parachute to safety;

It resembled a huge toy, but when assembled and inflated, it could carry two men and fly.

after the hole was patched the plane was pumped back up and flew again. The second case was tragic. An army test pilot over-stressed the wings during a flight, and the same thing happened: his wings folded into the propeller and deflated. In this case, part of the motor suddenly hit the pilot in the head, and though he was able to eject, his chute never opened, and he was killed. The project was suspended following the death of the army pilot.

But Ernest Stadvec of Barberton, who has written two books on the Inflatoplane and its history, says the idea was a good one that was never really given a chance. He calls it "one of aviation's might-have-beens." He feels that the safety issues could have been addressed and corrected.

He points out that Goodyear had invented a little airplane that the average person might have been able to store in an automobile trunk. Goodyear had proved it could be easily assembled, inflated, and flown, then deflated and packed up. He feels that it was just ahead of its time.

A total of twelve of the Inflatoplanes were built, and they continued testing them until 1972, when the project was finally scrapped. The Ohio Historical Society in Columbus has one of the actual planes as well as video footage showing the test flights. Sadly, the plane is in storage and not on display.

The Military Air Preservation Society at Akron-Canton Airport has asked the Ohio Historical Society to give the Inflatoplane to them so they can display it in their museum.

You Can't Get There from Main Street

ALLIANCE

A lot of almanacs and trivia books have had fun over the years at the expense of the good people of Alliance, Ohio.

Okay. Yes. It's true. Main Street in downtown Alliance starts at a dead-end street and goes, guess where? To another dead-end street—giving Alliance the questionable honor of being perhaps the only town in America whose main street doesn't go anywhere.

Usually the main street in a community is a continuation of a main highway that connects the town with other communities.

But no one ever offers an explanation of why this strange situation happened in Alliance.

Margaret Albright of the reference department at the Rodman Public Library in Alliance has a ready answer when asked, though.

She admits it is a fact that Main Street dead-ends on Sawburg Avenue at one end of the street and Webb Avenue at the other end. You have to twist and turn several times to reach a main highway to drive out of town. However, she also points to the fact that Alliance was founded in a time when railroads were the principal means of transportation and that the city of Alliance was located at the junction of two railroad rights of way. Ms. Albright says, "From this railroad crossing, the first streets were laid out, extending west."

So Main Street, which was the "main" street in the town, followed the railroad tracks west until stopping at a point just short of where one railroad turns south. In recent years Main Street has been extended farther west through Alliance's industrial park.

So there you have it. Alliance founders were not playing a practical joke on future motorists. Main Street was put where it was for the convenience of people who rode the train, which at that time was the most convenient and direct way to get in and out of town.

Rodman Public Library, 215 E. Broadway Street, Alliance, Ohio 44601, 330-821-2665, www.rodmanlibrary.com

The Painting That Went to Jail
BERLIN

Believe it or not, a painting was once "imprisoned" in the Holmes County, Ohio, jail.

That painting, titled *Behalt*, is unusual for another reason: it is 10 feet high and 265 feet long! It took artist Heinz Gaugel more than fourteen years to create. There are only three others like it in the world.

The story began in the 1960s when Gaugel, who was born and raised in Germany but had immigrated to Canada, was on a visit to Holmes County in Ohio. Gaugel had never heard of the Amish-Mennonite people who live in Ohio but was instantly taken when he met them and discovered they spoke his native language. The more he learned about the Amish and their disdain for modern trappings like automobiles, television, and radio, the more he was fascinated. Gaugel had a studio in Ontario, and he had already done a huge mural for a building near the Welland Canal. Now he had a new dream: to create the history of a people on canvas.

Because of religious beliefs, the Amish do not have any photographs of themselves or their families. Gaugel decided to create a larger-than-life mural that would trace the history of the Amish, Mennonites, and Hutterites from their earliest days in Europe to the present time. The enormity of the research alone was staggering. To further complicate matters, the local Amish people were suspicious of an outsider like Gaugel, despite the fact that he could speak the Pennsylvania Dutch language they used among themselves.

Undaunted, Gaugel moved into a home near Charm, Ohio, in the heart of the world's largest Amish community, and started quietly doing his research, even making a trip to Europe to learn more about the Anabaptist movement. He also sought out some church members whose ancestors had not moved to the United States so he could study their faces for his painting.

In 1978 Gaugel took over an old, unused frame church building in Berlin and began his masterpiece. He stretched huge blank canvases around the room and, using a ten-foot-long pole with a piece of chalk attached to it, sketched above the figures he would later paint. Asked once why he did not use a ladder or scaffolding, he replied with a twinkle in his eye, "When I am drawing I get so involved that I might forget and step off the ladder or the scaffold." Instead, by sketching from the ground, he could step back and immediately see if his drawings were in proper perspective.

As the weeks and months went by, the painting began to take on form and color, bringing to life historic scenes such as Martin Luther and the Reformation, the bloody persecution of the Anabaptists, and Christ's crucifixion. As the painting grew, more and more local people, including the Amish, came to watch. Trust be-

Gaugel painted from the floor using a long stick with charcoal on the end, because he was afraid of falling off scaffolding if he stepped back to admire his work.

gan to grow between the artist and the Amish. Bishops of the various Amish churches would suggest bits of their history that should be included in the painting. Soon Amish schools in the vicinity were making field trips to watch Heinz Gaugel paint their history.

He had completed about one hundred feet of the mural in 1979 when tragedy struck. His primary financial backer for the project, Helen Smucker, died. Ownership of the mural became an issue between Gaugel and Smucker's heirs. They accused Gaugel of trying to damage the huge mural. The conflict became so heated that lawsuits were filed, and the Holmes County sheriff intervened, confiscating the painting that the two sides were fighting over. The sheriff had no place else to put the enormous artwork but the county jail, and so it was stored in an unused cell under lock and key, becoming the first artwork in America to ever be imprisoned.

The fight continued in the courts for almost another year until April 1981, when a settlement was finally reached. Gaugel regained ownership of the painting with the stipulation he could not call it *Behalt* (meaning "to keep or remember"), the name he had chosen for it. (His opponents had formed a corporation called Behalt and even built a circular building on State Route 39 to display the cycloramic painting when it was completed.)

The painting that Heinz Gaugel envisioned telling the history of the Amish and Mennonites would become the third-largest cyclorama in the world.

Gaugel announced that he was renaming the painting *Legacy* and moving it to Lancaster, Pennsylvania, site of the second-largest Amish community in the country. There he planned to finish the project.

That's exactly what he did—almost. The painting was moved to Pennsylvania, and Gaugel did continue to work on it, but health problems from a heart attack, coupled with a serious traffic accident that severely injured one of his sons, took Gaugel away from the painting for nearly eight years.

It was in 1988 that a group planning to build a Mennonite information center in Berlin, Ohio, approached Gaugel. They offered him a way to bring the mural back to Ohio and a place in which to complete it. He accepted, and studios were built for him in the new center, constructed less than a half mile from where Gaugel had originally started painting the historic canvas.

Gaugel finally finished the enormous work in 1993. He also oversaw the construction of the large room at the Mennonite information center where his work would be exhibited. The final painting was 10 feet tall and 265 feet long. Only three other cycloramas in the world are larger. Gaugel's masterpiece was renamed *Behalt*. The court battles were over. The once-imprisoned painting was back home.

Heinz Gaugel died on December 28, 2000. His studio is preserved as a memorial to him at the Amish-Mennonite Heritage Center.

Amish-Mennonite Heritage Center (formerly Mennonite Information Center) County Route 77, Berlin, Ohio 44610, 330-893-3192.

Those Crooked Bridges

CAMBRIDGE

Why would anyone want to build a crooked bridge?

Early settlers sometimes did, and several such bridges can still be found in West Virginia, Pennsylvania, and Ohio. More commonly called "S bridges," they were designed by early bridge builders who found they could economically cross a stream, particularly one that the road hit on an angle, by making their bridge with curves.

It took less material, and time, to build a bridge shaped like an S so that the road crossed the stream at a true perpendicular, making the actual water crossing much shorter and, therefore, less expensive. However, this was in the days of horses and wagons, not fast-moving automobiles. Many of these bridges survived well into the twentieth century, and the walls bear the latter-day scars caused by motorists who suddenly, at high speed, found themselves fishtailing across the curvy bridges.

The best examples can be found along the old "National Road" that ran from western Pennsylvania through West Virginia and into Ohio. We found two of the bridges still standing but now cordoned off as roadside parks, no longer carrying traffic.

Old U.S. Route 40 (the National Road) between Cambridge and New Concord, Ohio.

Obviously people didn't travel very fast in the days when early road builders built "S" bridges over a river or stream.

The Frenchmen's Lost Gold
MINERVA

There have long been legends of gold, silver, or other treasure buried in Ohio. Most are just that. Legends.

For example, renegade frontiersman Simon Girty (known as "The White Savage" because he fought on the side of the Indians against early settlers) is believed to have buried loot in a number of places. The most persistent story concerns land where Girty once ran a trading post, a place now called Girty's Island at a bend in the Maumee River on Route 24, about seven miles from the Defiance State Park.

Near Delaware, Ohio, there was an Indian attack on a stagecoach purported to be carrying a strongbox filled with gold. The incident happened just south of the present Perkins Observatory site. Supposedly, the Indians had little use for the gold and buried it somewhere in the area.

Then there was the legend of a farmer named Geyer, near Alton, Ohio. It was the late 1800s, and the farmer distrusted banks. He also didn't trust his wife and secreted lots of money on his farm. Allegedly, he was murdered by a hired hand, but the money was never found.

During the War of 1812 it was rumored that an army payroll was hidden near, or even inside, Fort Findlay. It was hidden just prior to an Indian raid, and in the fighting the officer who hid the money was killed and the location never discovered.

But one story, the legend of the missing Frenchmen's gold, might just be a bit more than just wishful thinking. It's a tale filled with tantalizing facts that tease the imagination.

The story starts out much like some of the others, with a long-ago war and a lost or hidden cache of money. There are several versions, but most agree that somewhere between 1755 and 1758, the French who then occupied Fort Duquesne, which today is Pittsburgh, Pennsylvania, were threatened by advancing British troops. Since they were a major force on what was then the frontier, they had a sizable amount of gold and silver on hand to pay their troops and to use in trading with pioneers. The British advance was so sudden and fast that the decision was made to move the fort's treasure to another location. It was decided to take it all the way across the Ohio country to Fort Detroit at the western end of Lake Erie.

A squad of ten men with sixteen pack horses carrying gold and silver and supplies set out across what was then called the "Great Trail," a path roughly paralleling today's U.S. Route 30. They had reached somewhere between East Rochester and Malvern, Ohio, near present-day Minerva, Ohio, when they thought they heard British coming down the trail. Fearing they were outnumbered, they panicked and quickly unloaded the pack animals and buried the boxes of gold and silver, making notes of landmarks nearby so they could find the spot after the British were out of sight.

They had just finished the task and had returned to the trail when out of the woods came a column of British redcoats. In a swift but brutal fight, all but two of the French soldiers were killed.

One of the two ended up an American citizen, living in North Carolina. In 1829, nearly seventy years after the battle, a nephew of the French soldier found a letter among his uncle's possessions that included clues as to where the treasure had been buried. It sounded like a pirate's map: they were to look for the figure of a deer carved in a tree. Another landmark was a stone wedged in the fork of a tree. The shovels to dig the hole for the treasure had also been buried under a log. The area, near Minerva, was on land where there was a group of natural springs.

The French soldier's nephew came to Minerva and started searching. But as local folks answered his questions and realized just what he was searching for, the assistance he was getting suddenly stopped. If there was treasure located in or near Minerva, the local folks wanted to find it for themselves. After a few frustrating days of misdirections and a growing feeling that he was not wanted in the community, the soldier's nephew gave up and returned to North Carolina. As soon as he was out of sight, a mini–gold rush started in Minerva. People began digging holes in their yards, and they scoured their farms and the surrounding countryside looking for the clues the Frenchman's nephew had told them about. But nothing was found.

Down through the years, new efforts to locate the treasure would be launched, and, amazingly, some of the clues were discovered.

In 1949 Elson Robbins, who owned a farm near Minerva, took a newspaper reporter from the *Canton Repository* to an area of natural springs on his property. He said that when he was a boy, two crossed, French-made shovels had been found in a hole beneath a log. He claimed to have used the shovels for many years. He also claimed to have seen a faded carving of a deer in an ancient tree. Others apparently also saw it when the tree was cut down. It stood one mile east of the springs. A half mile west, another old tree was discovered to have a stone embedded in the fork of its trunk. It had been there so long that bark had grown over it. Another farmer, John Whitacre, made that discovery on his farm.

Over the years, other archaeological excavations have uncovered the remains of a soldier and his equipment not far from these sites. There have also been discoveries of bullets and other equipment from the time period in which the treasure is said to have disappeared. Something certainly did happen here.

Over time, interest in the lost gold faded. But every once in a while someone makes another attempt to find the location. Minerva even holds a "Lost Gold Festival." Most local folks agree that the springs referred to in the old French soldier's letter were Beaver Hat Spring and Cranberry Spring. The actual area the treasure is thought to be buried in is southwest of the intersection of Augusta and Ridge Roads in Minerva.

But before you grab a shovel and head for Minerva, there are a couple of things you should bear in mind: Most of the sites are on private property, so you can't go there without permission. And, probably more important, remember that there were *two* survivors of the battle. No one ever heard from the other Frenchman. Perhaps the reason no one has been able to find the treasure is that he came back after the battle, dug up the treasure boxes, and disappeared into the mists of history.

Ohio's First Traffic Fatality

NORWICH

Christopher Columbus Baldwin secured a place in American history. Two places, actually. That second chance at fame, though, he might have preferred to miss.

Baldwin was the second librarian of the American Antiquarian Society, a group that built and still maintains a national library of American history literature and culture.

He served from 1827 to 1835 and was personally responsible for obtaining thousands of works for the library from early American authors and publishers.

It was in the pursuit of this work that Baldwin gained a second kind of fame: Christopher Columbus Baldwin became Ohio's first known traffic fatality.

In 1835 the American Antiquarian Society, headquartered in Massachusetts, ordered Baldwin to head out to the Ohio Frontier to investigate some recently discovered ancient American Indian burial mounds in southern Ohio.

Speed was blamed in Ohio's first recorded traffic fatality, when a stagecoach rolled over near this spot.

There weren't many ways to travel to Ohio in those days. Either you went by riverboat from Pittsburgh down the Ohio River, or by boat from Buffalo on Lake Erie to one of the Ohio ports, like Cleveland, or you took your chances on the National Road, which stretched from the east coast to the Mississippi Valley. The National Road, built by the federal government during Thomas Jefferson's presidency, was in some places a road in name only.

An author named Charles Fenno Hoffman described his ride on the National Road in 1833 this way: "The ruts are worn so broad and deep by heavy travel that an army of pygmies might march into the bosom of the country under the cover they provide!"

It was on the National Road (today U.S. 40), that Christopher Columbus Baldwin chose to make his trek, by stagecoach, to southern Ohio.

On August 20, 1835, while speeding down a winding hill into the village of Norwich, the stagecoach ran off the road at a curve and rolled over. When rescuers reached the wreckage of the coach, they found the 35-year-old Baldwin inside, dead.

A stone and bronze tablet, perhaps the only monument to commemorate a traffic accident, was erected at the site in 1925 by the Norwich Boy Scout Troop, commemorating the man who became the Buckeye State's first traffic fatality.

The memorial stone is located on old U.S. Route 40 at the eastern end of the village of Norwich, on the north side of the road at a sharp curve.

Fort Fizzle

GLENMONT

The movie *Gangs of New York* depicts the resistance to the military draft during the American Civil War in the 1860s. The bloody battle in the movie is based on the little-known fact that there was much division in the country about the war at that time.

Perhaps one of Ohio's best-kept secrets is the armed rebellion that occurred in one of the Buckeye State's most unlikely places: bucolic Holmes County.

History tells us that during the Civil War more soldiers came out of Holmes County, per capita, than any other county in Ohio. However, there were also many from Holmes County who opposed the conflict, who considered themselves "Peace Democrats."

Those supporting the war called them "Copperheads," intimating that they really favored the Southern cause.

In 1863 one of the nation's first draft laws was passed. It called for the conscription of all Northern men between the ages of 20 and 45 into the Union army.

It did not take long for resistance to arise.

The Copperheads protested the draft and did it so loudly that army

All that remains of Fort Fizzle, the site of Ohio's only armed rebellion during the Civil War, is this pile of stones.

troops had to be called in to escort and protect officers who were trying to enforce the law.

On Friday, June 5, 1863, Ohio's rebellion started with a rock being thrown.

A federal officer came from Loudonville to Holmes County to see how the draft was working. He was hit in the head with a rock thrown by a man who was later identified as Peter Stuber. Another man, William Greiner, pulled a pistol and fired it in the air. That was enough for the federal man; he skedaddled out of town, alone.

Soon after, a no-nonsense army captain, James Drake, who was the U.S. provost marshal, arrived with seven men and arrested Peter Stuber and three other men. Stuber admitted throwing the rock but claimed he didn't know the man was a federal officer; he said he thought the officer was just a stranger in town to "stir up trouble."

Captain Drake and his men had started toward Wooster with their prisoners when they were surprised by a mob that included eight to ten armed men. The mob surrounded federal officials and demanded they throw down their weapons and hand over the shackled men. Drake and his men did so reluctantly and then rode out of town alone.

This action brought the situation to a boiling point. In a very short time hundreds of Copperhead supporters, all armed with shotguns and pitchforks, had gathered in the tiny town of Napoleon, which today goes by the name of Glenmont. They were determined to turn back any further efforts by federal officials to enforce the conscription law.

Word of the gathering reached Columbus and the Ohio adjutant general's office, which immediately ordered a battalion of 450 men along with an additional group identified as "20 squirrel hunters from Wooster and some sharpshooters from Dennison" to start heading for Holmes County. When word that an armed group of soldiers under the command of Colonel William Wallace was on the way filtered back to Holmes County, a majority of the Copperheads decided they perhaps had urgent business elsewhere and went back home. Only a handful of Peace Democrats were left to face the approaching military.

The insurgents wisely decided not to attempt to stop the approaching soldiers on the road but to make their stand just a few miles southeast of present-day Glenmont. There stood a stone house on a farm. They took this over and christened it Fort Vallandigham, in honor of their congressman, the well-known Copperhead Clement Vallandigham. Somewhere they came up with four cannons and some small arms. They thought they were well positioned. The old stone house even had a well in the basement and a tunnel that led to a nearby orchard.

However, as the Union troops started to arrive by foot, wagon, and buggy, many of the participants in the rebellion began to get cold feet.

As the Union troops formed up and marched in a steady line toward "Fort Vallandigham," the nervous insurgents suddenly fired a ragged volley at them. Every shot missed.

The Union forces stopped, leveled their rifles at the fort, and returned the fire.

They too, missed. An officer gave orders to the Union troops to fix bayonets and then yelled "Charge!!!"

The line of blue came running toward the "fort."

A poem published in a local newspaper after the battle best summed up what happened next:

Their leader, he got panic struck
And said he'd been mistaken.
And told them, "Run with all your might
And try to save your bacon."

Another eyewitness said it was like watching a "flock of quail taking flight."

The Copperheads turned tail and started running out windows and doorways of the "fort" into the nearby woods and hills. The battle was over.

Some reports say the actual battle lasted only a minute, perhaps five at the most.

A couple of the insurgents were wounded, but it's not known whether that was from all the bullets flying around, a bayonet wound, or just simply a clumsy fall on some rocks as they tried to run away.

As for Peter Stuber, who threw the rock that started the whole thing, and the other three men who were involved, they surrendered to Colonel Wallace and were later freed after taking a pledge not to take up arms against the Union again. Ironically, Stuber was later drafted, and this time he went into the army peacefully as a private, served two months, and was honorably discharged.

As stories about the Holmes County rebellion began to spread, news reports started referring to "Fort Vallandigham" as "Fort Fizzle," since the battle had fizzled. The name stuck, and ever since the fight has been known as the Battle of Fort Fizzle.

Today, the site of the state's only armed rebellion is on private property near the intersections of County Roads 6 and 25, near Glenmont. The present owner told me he hopes someday to open the site to the public. All that remains is a spring, the tunnel that was to have been the defenders' escape route, and the stone foundation of what was once Fort Fizzle.

The Lincoln Hoax

MANSFIELD

Many great stories turn out to be urban legends. You know, a story that seems very plausible and has been told and retold with such sincerity that you think it must be true, but in the end it turns out not to be.

But some such stories just refuse to die. Take the Abraham Lincoln story from Mansfield, Ohio, for example.

There is a bronze plaque in the park in downtown Mansfield that proclaims, "The first public and official endorsement of Abraham Lincoln as candidate for President of the United States was given him in Mansfield at a county convention held November 5, 1858." This plaque was erected by the Richland County Lincoln Association.

The authenticity of this event is borne out by the files of the *Sandusky Daily Commercial Register,* which on Saturday morning, November 6, 1858, ran a front-page story that read:

> Lincoln for President.
> We are indebted to a friend at Mansfield for the following special dispatch: "Editor Sandusky Register: An enthusiastic meeting is in progress here tonight in favor of Lincoln for the new Republican Candidate for President."

Now understand, this was 1858, years before the next presidential election, and if Abraham Lincoln was planning a run for the presidency, no one else knew about it. He had served as a congressman and had even been mentioned as a vice-presidential candidate in the previous election, but nothing had come of that.

This story about a Mansfield convention was picked up by other newspapers all over the country, and it's believed that it was responsible for the renewed interest in the man from Illinois.

The story created enough curiosity that the Eastern power brokers finally invited the little-known Illinois attorney and former congressman to come speak in New York so they could see what the fuss was all about. One of the talks Lincoln gave on that tour was the famous Cooper Union speech that put him on the main track for the presidency in 1860.

But did Lincoln himself really believe that a small-town meeting in Ohio was the catalyst that started him on the road to the presidency?

Apparently so. According to Dr. Roger Bridges, former executive director of the Hayes Presidential Center in Fremont, Lincoln, while president, had a meeting with Mansfield businessman Thomas Webster, Jr., in which he said, "Mansfield is a great place. It was that town that first saw my fitness for the presidency."

It's a wonderful story: a tiny town in central Ohio shaping our national destiny simply because residents there had the foresight to recognize Lincoln's greatness before anyone else. It gave proof to the fact that every voice in this country can be heard, even from the smallest communities.

Does this statue commemorate a huge practical joke, or did Mansfield really become the first city in America to call for Abraham Lincoln to run for president?

There's only one problem: The meeting that sparked all the interest in Lincoln may have never happened.

The short story in the *Commercial Register* did not come to light until many years after Lincoln's death. When it did there was great excitement.

It was decided that a monument committee be formed for the construction of a suitable memorial to the event that made Mansfield one of the cradles of Lincoln's presidency. It was even suggested that some of the people who took part in the convention might still be around and could also take part in the dedication ceremony. The first indication that everything may not have been as it appeared was that while there were some members of the community old enough to have been around in 1858, no one remembered a convention on that date that had anything to do with politics or Abraham Lincoln.

In fact, when the committee turned to the files of the *Mansfield Herald*, the local newspaper, which, incidentally, was a staunchly Republican paper, to see what they had written about the convention, they found the only meeting in town that was covered was a gathering of railroad owners from around the country. Not a line was written about Abraham Lincoln.

To add to the mystery, they continued to search later editions of the paper, hoping to find some mention of the Lincoln gathering, when one of the searchers discovered that in the *Mansfield Herald* edition of November 6, 1858, the day after the convention was supposed to have been held, right in the middle of the front page was a gaping hole. Someone had cut an article out of the paper. Since this was before microfilm and computers, this aging newspaper was thought to be the only record still left of that day in the community. And perhaps the missing article had something to do with the Lincoln meeting.

A local book dealer had an inspiration. There was one other repository of many of the early newspapers, the Ohio Historical Society in Columbus. A trip there quickly turned up another copy of the November 6, 1858, *Mansfield Herald*, and there, on the front page, was the missing story. The story that had been cut out of the Mansfield newspaper was about Abraham Lincoln, but it wasn't the story the folks in Mansfield expected.

It read: "Mansfield is a large city and many great occurrences doubtless take place in it which we never heard of, yet we are inclined to think that a large and enthusiastic political meeting would be likely to come to our knowledge. Under the circumstances we are rather disposed to consider the Register's Lincoln demonstration somewhat imaginary. THE TRUTH IS, THE REGISTER HAS BEEN HOAXED." There had been no convention about Lincoln, political or otherwise.

The local Lincoln group that had planned the monument had a problem.

Probably more than a few of them began to think that the story was a practical joke. But on the other hand, even though the meeting was never held, the erroneous report had been spread all over the country, and even Lincoln believed it was responsible for his renewed popularity, if not his nomination as president. Maybe it was better to just let sleeping dogs lie.

The monument was built, and Mansfield to this day can lay claim to being the first place in the nation to call for Lincoln as president.

Even though it may have never happened.

Why did the Sandusky newspaper stage the hoax? No one is quite certain. But some writers have pointed to David Ross Locke, an Ohio newspaperman who created a humorous character called "Petroleum V. Nasby" in the *Toledo Blade*. There is some evidence that he was in Mansfield on the night of November 5, 1858. Locke was a man known for a love of practical jokes, and he was a friend of the *Mansfield Herald*'s editor. The whole thing might have just been a prank that they attempted to play on the editor of the Sandusky paper, also a friend. A prank that may have unknowingly contributed to the election of one of America's most beloved presidents.

Down through the years a few historians have tried to make the case that the Mansfield meeting really did happen, offering names of five prominent citizens who later claimed to have been there. There have also been claims that the editor of the Mansfield paper claimed the meeting never happened because he was pledged to support another Republican, Salmon P. Chase, governor of Ohio and a presidential hopeful. Still others have asked, if there was a meeting, why wasn't it reported in other area newspapers of the day?

Whether it happened or not is probably not as important today as the fact that Lincoln and many others across the country did believe the story, and it helped change American history.

Cleveland's Big Party

CLEVELAND

In 1936 the city of Cleveland, Ohio, gave a party. It lasted two years, and seven million people showed up.

It was the height of the Great Depression; thousands were still out of work. The federal government was trying "alphabet" economics, with such organizations as the WPA, the PWA, the NRA, and dozens of other programs to get the economy going again.

The Cleveland party was called the Great Lakes Exposition, and while it wasn't officially a world's fair, it certainly had all the trappings and hoopla of a world-class event. And believe it or not, the whole thing was put together in less than a year.

One of the many attractions at the Great Lakes Exposition in 1937 was a giant water show staged on the lakefront where the Science Center is located today.

Officially it was the Cleveland Centennial and Great Lakes Exposition, celebrating the one-hundredth anniversary of the date that Cleveland had become a city. Credit for the idea of the exposition is given to Frank J. Ryan and Leon Dickey, who was Cleveland's first commissioner of Public Hall. But it took the leadership of a wealthy Clevelander, Dudley S. Blossom, to really get the project under way. Blossom held the chairmanship of a committee of movers and shakers in the community, and together they raised $1.5 million in local funds to start drawing plans and constructing the exposition grounds.

In just under eight months two hundred buildings were born on a 125-acre lakefront site. The grounds sprawled from Public Hall to the then new Municipal Stadium on the lakefront and to near East 22nd Street to the east.

The grand entrance was at East Sixth Street near Public Hall, on Lakeside Avenue. The entryway swept toward the lake, lined with two-story-high silver eagle pylons. It was called "The Court of Presidents," honoring men from the Great Lakes area who had served as president of the United States.

Even President Franklin Delano Roosevelt stopped in on August 14, 1936, to take a look and congratulate the city on bringing the community together to build the fair.

From a vantage point on the mall above, looking toward the lake, especially at night, it resembled some futuristic city, with pulsing music, colored lights stabbing into the darkness, and the flow of thousands of people.

"It was just beautiful. You just couldn't believe it was Cleveland," recalls 96-year-old H. B. "Army" Armstrong of Bay Village, Ohio. Armstrong and his wife, Guyanna, were newlyweds when the exposition on the lakefront opened.

"The lakefront around East Ninth Street was the city dump at the time. It was a smelly mess," Armstrong said. "And in a matter of months they brought truckload after truckload of dirt in, paved it over, and built the exposition where they used to burn garbage."

At the top of the entrance, as you looked toward the lake on the left, was the stadium. Public Hall had been turned into Radioland, and broadcast greats of the day, like *Fibber McGee and Molly*, would originate their network programs from the Exposition. In the foreground was the outdoor-exhibit building and a great band shell that offered concerts sponsored by the Sherwin Williams Company. Not far away was a building operated by Western Reserve University where you could watch scientists at work. The Horticultural Gardens filled the area between the stadium and the lake with beautiful walkways surrounded by flowers and plants from all over. Nearby was the Hall of Progress, with acres of cars and industrial and governmental exhibits.

On the right side of the plaza was Winterland, a complex for wintertime sports such as ice skating and ice shows. An exotic Florida exhibit featured orange groves, fountains, and even a southern-style colonial home. Higbee's department store had its exhibit located in the tallest structure in the exposition, the Tower of Light. The Firestone Building had its entryway guarded by singing fountains that, at night, changed color in tempo to the recorded music played through loudspeakers in each fountain. Inside, a farm exhibit complete with animals and farm equipment demonstrated Firestone products.

Standard Drug had a 120-foot-long working soda fountain in their exhibit.

Docked at the water's edge were two very special ships, Admiral Richard Byrd's sailing ship that he took to Antarctica and one of the U.S. Navy's latest submarines at that time, the S-49. Both were open for public inspection.

Spread out where Voinovich Park and the Rock and Roll Hall of Fame are today was the amusement section with all kinds of carnival rides and sideshow events. There were speedboat rides on the lake and theaters with various stage shows. Just past the midway was another exhibit called Streets of the World. It was a ten-acre international village that brought together people from forty nationalities to demonstrate cultures and foods. It was one of the most popular attractions at the show.

Like many folks, the newlywed Armstrongs found the Great Lakes Exposition a welcome relief from the drabness of the Depression years. Army was a teacher in the Cleveland Public Schools; Guyanna worked as a photographer's model.

"We didn't have much money, but we managed to go to the exposition several times each week. It was just plain fun," Armstrong said. "We usually went in the evening, for the shows, dancing, and nightclubs. Oh, and also the grapefruit wine. I don't remember which pavilion offered it but it was very good, and it must have been cheap, because we drank it every night we went there."

In 1937 New York show biz entrepreneur Billy Rose came to the Great Lakes Exposition and rebuilt the lakefront Marine Theater, which had been one of the main exposition attractions the previous year. He called it Billy Rose's Aquacade, and his stars included former Olympians Johnny Weissmuller, who would later go on to play Tarzan in the movies, and Eleanor Holmes, whom Rose would eventually marry.

"It was a choreographed swimming show with music and comedy. The audience sat in an amphitheater dining room on the edge of the water where the Science Center is today," Armstrong remembers. "The stage was on a floating barge out in the harbor. They had to dump barrels of chlorine into the water each day before the show to protect the swimmers. That's how dirty Lake Erie was then."

While the exposition was filled with lots of cultural attractions, the Armstrongs, like most people in their twenties and thirties, visited the big show mostly for the entertainment.

"In the amusement section they had a live show with several 250-pound ballerinas," Armstrong remembers. "What surprised us was that despite their size, they were very good. We went back to see them several times."

Without a doubt, the midway section of the Great Lakes Exposition was probably the most popular with the majority of visitors. There were new state-of-the-art carnival-style rides, along with the usual sideshow attractions.

"They had one exhibit that was called Graham's Midgets," said Armstrong. "It was like a miniature circus, and all the performers were little people." (One of the performers was Meinhard Raabe, who in the next year would star as the Munchkin Coroner who pronounces the wicked witch dead in the movie *The Wizard of Oz*.)

"I had a white suit at the time, and when Guyanna saw it, she decided she wanted one too," Armstrong recalled. "So we went to a tailor and had him make a white suit for Guyanna, and we both wore white suits one evening when we went to the Exposition.

"We stopped at an attraction called the Bouquet of Life. It had all these glass jars with what were said to be baby embryos, and a woman wearing a nurse's uniform was giving a lecture on the stages of the development of life. I suppose we asked a couple of questions—it was pretty interesting—when right in the middle of her presentation the nurse stopped and said, 'That's it! You're just putting me on. I know you are doctors!' Guyanna and I laughed all evening about that one. It must have been those white suits."

The Goodyear Blimp was docked to the west of the entertainment area on land that today houses Burke Lakefront Airport. If you could afford it, you could take a short ride in the blimp along the water's edge and see a bird's-eye view of the exposition.

But by far the most curious exhibit at the Great Lakes Exposition was a death mask made from the head of a murdered man.

Eliot Ness, yes, that Eliot Ness, the former "untouchable" from Chicago, was then Cleveland's safety director and was embroiled in the search for a serial murderer who was leaving decapitated and dismembered bodies in junk-littered lots around the town. The latest victim had turned up in Kingsbury Run near the East 55th Street Bridge. Two young boys made the grisly discovery of the head of a white male, wrapped in a pair of trousers.

The next day police found the rest of the man's body near the Nickel Plate Railroad Police Office. Despite a good set of fingerprints obtained from the remains, and the fact that the dead man had six distinctive tattoos on his body, detectives were unable to identify him.

It was decided, with Eliot Ness's approval, to make a plaster death mask of the man and put it on display, along with a diagram of the tattoos, at the Great Lakes Exposition in hopes that somebody would recognize the murderer's latest victim.

Although thousands and thousands of visitors to the exposition saw the death mask, no one was able to say who the victim was. The case was never solved.

"Why did we go to the exposition so often?" Armstrong said. "Well, it was fun, it wasn't terribly expensive—it couldn't have been, we didn't have much money—and it was so big, there was just no way you could see it all in a day, or even a few days."

The Armstrongs saw their first television at the Great Lakes Exposition in 1937. In the Varied Industries Building was one of the first television cameras, and it was connected to a floor model TV that produced a picture of about fourteen inches. Visitors could walk in front of the camera and see themselves in flickering black and white on the nearby TV set.

There was also the GE exhibit, where visitors to the exposition could throw a switch and light up the world's largest light bulb, a 50,000-watt giant. Each participant was awarded a certificate proclaiming they had lit the bulb.

It was a show that was meant to establish bragging rights—from the world's biggest light bulb to the world's largest book. The book was called *The Golden Book of Cleveland*, and it measured five feet by seven feet. It contained six thousand pages for signatures of visitors to the exposition, and it weighed nearly two-and-a-half tons. Each signer got a gilded pamphlet with the page, column, and line where they had signed the big book.

Amazingly, no one knows what happened to the giant book after the exposition closed. News reports at the time indicated that the book would be given to a historical society. The Western Reserve Historical Society receives several inquiries about the book each year, but a search of the society's warehouse and artifacts has never located the exhibit. The Ohio Historical Society also knows of the book but has no record of receiving it. Perhaps *The Golden Book of Cleveland*, all two-and-a-half tons of it, is gathering dust in a Cleveland warehouse. Or, perhaps in a burst of patriotism during one of the many World War II scrap and paper drives, the book was donated to the war effort.

Whatever really happened to it, the whereabouts of *The Golden Book of Cleveland* remains one of the mysteries of the Great Lakes Exposition.

By late summer 1937 the Great Lakes Exposition was winding down. It had run a total of more than two hundred days and stretched over parts of two years. It had cost $1.5 million to build, and it pumped an estimated $77 million into the Cleveland economy during its run. More than seven million people had poured into Cleveland to be part of the city's biggest party.

That party officially closed on September 6, 1937.

Almost immediately, demolition crews moved in and started tearing down the buildings that had housed attractions like the Ripley's Believe It or Not Odditorium. The Florida Building and its orange trees disappeared, as did the chair once used by Confederate President Jefferson Davis. Monkeyland, where trained simians had driven little cars to entertain the visitors, was no more. Also falling to the wrecker's hammers was a replica of Shake-

Everyone who signed the huge Golden Book of Cleveland got a miniature booklet describing what page and line his or her name was on, but at seven feet tall, five feet wide, containing six thousand pages, and weighing more than two tons, how could the original have been misplaced?

speare's Globe Theatre and a reproduction of Charles Dickens's Old Curiosity Shop. The rickshaws and the roller chairs used to transport visitors were gone now, as were the college athletes who had been hired to provide the muscle to push them. The specially designed Greyhound Bus people movers had moved on. Some of the exhibits were crated up and moved to New York City for the upcoming opening of the 1939 World's Fair there.

By February 1938, just six months after the show closed, the buildings had vanished. Only concrete walkways and piles of rubble remained.

"I remember going to a West Side lumber dealer in the spring of 1938 and seeing all kinds of doors, windows, and wood that had been salvaged from the exposition," said H. B. Armstrong. "It was kind of sad. Just a few months earlier it had been this beautiful, fun event, and now all that was left was some scrap lumber."

Cleveland Municipal Stadium was torn down in the 1990s to make way for the new Cleveland Browns Stadium.

The last exhibit from the show, the Donald Gray Horticultural Gardens, although much smaller than in the glory days of the exposition, had managed to cling to the north side of the old stadium. They were removed during the demolition, and while promises were made to re-create them with the new stadium, so far it hasn't happened.

The death mask of the murdered man seen by many of the visitors at the show is now in the Cleveland Police Museum in the Justice Center. No one ever identified him.

Many reports have credited the exposition with the creation of what has become Burke Lakefront Airport.

H. B. "Army" Armstrong taught in the Cleveland Public Schools for forty-seven years. He and Guyanna celebrated their fifty-fourth wedding anniversary before her death in 1991.

The Great Lakes Exposition of 1936–37 has disappeared into the pages of history. But it was a heck of a party while it lasted.

Racing Cows

BURTON

They call horse racing the Sport of Kings. So what do you call cow racing? That's right, cow racing.

I have seen dog races, sheep races, even pig races, but cow races?

It has indeed happened—at the Great Geauga County Fair in Burton, Ohio.

Cows don't run, you say? Well, if you've ever been on a farm trying to round up a young heifer who doesn't want to leave the pasture, you know that cows not only run, they can outrun a human.

In official cow racing, there are a few rules. First, no bull. I mean it, they do not allow bulls in their races, and only female cows are permitted. The race is on a one-mile course, but there's no penalty if the cow, during the race, stops to graze or wander into the infield.

Cows seem to have a mind of their own when it comes to racing. Some lope along in a fairly straight line and then get distracted and head for the fence or for a nearby watering trough despite the urging of the farmer-jockey on their back. Others just don't like to be told where to go. If the rider wants to go north, the cow will decide it wants to go south. Cows are also not accustomed to having saddles on their backs and have been known to leave the race to find a fence post so they can try to rub off the saddle—and anyone who might be sitting in it.

But if the race does go well and the cows stay reasonably on the track, or at least within the park itself, the big finale of the contest can also be a problem. I speak of crossing the finish line. Now, this may sound easy, but when you watch a race it turns out most of the entrants just don't get the idea of going through a line of cones at the end. Several usually have to be led through.

Now if you have ever spent any time around dairy cattle you probably know that when they get frisky and start running, you can usually stop or at least redirect them by stepping into their path. Cows, unlike bulls, buffalo, horses, goats, and even small children, won't try to run you down. They will usually turn away. Which explains some of the problems they have getting the cows to finally cross a finish line: that is the place where there are people milling around—judges,

You can lead a cow to water, but making her race is another story.

photographers with their cameras flashing, and, of course, the cheering crowd. It's enough to make the poor cow turn around and run back to the barn. Which some of them have been known to do.

Watching a cow race is what you might call an "udderly mooving" experience.

The couple that started the whole thing has a motto, "Don't milk them, race them." Pete Ondrus and his wife, Barb Lambert, of Carson City, Michigan, sold their five-hundred-head dairy farm herd in 1996 when they decided to retire from farming. They were looking for something fun to do that would include their knowledge of dairy cows. They decided that racing cows might be just what they were looking for and at the same time promote agriculture. So they founded the Mid-Michigan Cow Racing Association, known as the MMCRA, and then they also organized the World-Wide Cow Racing Association, or the WWCRA. (You know, everybody goes by initials these days.) They declared they would sponsor the "Udder Race."

In 2003 the Udder Race was won by a Vermont heifer by the name of Little Witch. She crossed the finish line in a blazing 7:31:54. By the way, Dusty Rhodes, owned by Ondrus and Lambert, came in a distant fifth in the race with a speed of 13:57:61. The jockey could have probably walked faster. In fact, that speed sounds a bit like the times turned in by caterpillars at Vermilion, Ohio's annual Woolly-bear Festival races. Which is about as fast as watching paint dry.

Cow racing may not compete with the Kentucky Derby or even Woollybear racing, but it does attract crowds. Geauga County Fair officials said that they've had several thousand people line up in advance to get the grandstand seats on the day of the cow races. Usually the crowd spills over all along the racetrack.

The jockeys are mostly area farmers who don't usually ride their cows. So perhaps that explains an apparent lack of control over the bovines. The breed seems to make little difference. Everything from a black-and-white Holstein to a buttermilk-colored Jersey heifer has been entered in the race. Size also doesn't seem to matter. Pete Ondrus's huge Holstein, Dusty Rhodes, has won her share of races, but at the event we witnessed she was left in the Geauga County dust by a smallish Guernsey heifer by the name of Starlite. And, as one jockey-farmer put it, "Even if the cow doesn't win you can still milk her . . . or even eat her."

As of this writing, it's uncertain whether the big event will continue to be featured at the Geauga County Fair. Cow-racing fans are advised to inquire before going.

The Great Geauga County Fair, P.O. Box 402, Burton, Ohio 44021, 440-834-1846, www.geaugafair.com

The World-Wide Cow Racing Association, c/o Pete Ondrus and Barb Lambert, 9517 South Warner Road, Carson City, Michigan 48611, 989-584-6286, www.cowrace.com

A Chair for God

BERLIN

God has a chair waiting for him in Holmes County.

In 1849 Jonas Stutzman, the first Amish settler to arrive in eastern Holmes County, published a booklet in which he predicted that God was about to return sometime within the next four years.

To get ready for the big event, Stutzman wore nothing but white clothing. He was so convinced God was coming that he built an oversized chair for the Lord's exclusive use. The chair was constructed with perfectly fitted parts, and not one nail was used in it.

Stutzman's forecast did not come true, but at one time he had

Jonas Stutzman was so certain that God would return to earth that he built a special chair for God to sit in.

many fellow believers.

An unusual man to the end, when he died in 1871 Stutzman requested that his body not to be carried by any kind of vehicle. So at his funeral his fellow church members formed two teams of pallbearers that alternated carrying his casket by hand, seven miles to the hillside family cemetery in Walnut Creek

You can see Stutzman and his chair depicted in the mural *Behalt* at the Amish-Mennonite Heritage Center in Berlin, Ohio. The actual chair that Stutzman built, "God's Chair," is also there on display at the center.

Behalt is one of only three cycloramic murals in the world and depicts the history of the Amish and Mennonite faiths. It was the work of artist Heinz Gaugel, who devoted the last third of his life to the giant painting. (See "The Painting That Went to Jail.")

Amish-Mennonite Heritage Center, 5798 County Road 77, Berlin, Ohio 44610, 330-893-3192.

The Biggest Flag

NORWALK

The VFW in Norwalk, Ohio, wanted to make a real splash during the bicentennial year of 1976. They wanted to create the largest flag in America. They succeeded. But they also created a flag so big that it can be flown only on especially calm days.

The flag, the largest to ever fly from a mast, is forty-six feet wide and seventy-seven feet long. When folded it weighs more than 120 pounds, and it has to be hauled to the flagpole in a special trailer, pulled by a small tractor.

The stars are each two feet across, and each stripe is four feet wide.

A tower that was specially built to display the flag was 150 feet high, and when the flag was flown at half-mast it almost touched the ground.

It didn't take long to figure out the problem with its size. VFW members tell about one day when they were raising or lowering the giant flag and a crew of fifteen to twenty men was trying to assist. "A sudden gust of wind hit the flag while I was holding on real tight," one man told me, "and the next thing I knew I was flying twenty feet off the ground!" His team members, seeing his distress, quickly lowered the flag to bring him gently back to earth.

The flag is flown, weather permitting, on Veterans Day, the Fourth of July, and other special occasions.

On Veterans Day 2003, disaster struck. The flag had just been raised when a wind suddenly arose, and before anyone could get to the flagpole the giant flag had

It takes a crew of twenty people just to raise and lower this flag.

toppled the 150-foot tower and also pulled down a baseball backstop. When they finally untangled the huge flag from the twisted wreckage of the tower and the backstop, they discovered that the flag was badly damaged. The Norwalk Furniture Company came to their rescue and helped repair the flag, but the tower is still down at this writing, and the VFW is holding a fund drive to build a bigger and, hopefully, much stronger tower from which to display the flag.

Norwalk Veterans of Foreign Wars, 140 Milan Avenue, Norwalk, Ohio 44857, 419-668-2335.

The Legend of Chester Bedell
BERLIN

Chester Bedell of Berlin Township in Portage County was a contrary man, a man who did not like to be pushed to do anything. Some folks claim he was so contrary that after his death his grave has been infested with snakes of all sizes and shapes. Why snakes? Read on . . .

Bedell, a very successful farmer in the late nineteenth century, owned thousands of acres of land. By some reports he was a kind man who donated many things to his community. In fact, Bedell Road near Berlin Center is named for him.

Yet in the last years of his life Chester Bedell did something that outraged many of his neighbors and caused so much controversy in this northeastern Ohio community that some residents still don't like to discuss the matter.

Then, when he died in 1908 at the age of 82, his grave became a local legend.

According to Ivan Hoyle, a member of the Berlin Township Historical Society, Bedell's problems began with his marriage to a woman of another faith. (Bedell had been raised a Methodist, and his wife was a Presbyterian.) It seems Bedell's father-in-law decided that Chester should change religions. When he refused, the father-in-law had Bedell's son baptized by a Presbyterian minister when Chester was not around. This infuriated Bedell and touched off a lifelong battle with his in-laws that included many lawsuits (all of which Bedell repeatedly claimed he won).

The family battle was bad enough, then Bedell went and proclaimed that he didn't believe in the stories of the Bible. This was shocking news in a rural society that was mostly made up of Methodists and Presbyterians. Ivan Hoyle isn't sure whether Chester started making these statements because he truly was an atheist or because he was simply pushing some buttons to upset his in-laws, who were devout Presbyterians.

Chester had made two trips to the Holy Land to trace the footsteps of Jesus, looking for proof of his existence, and he reportedly came home both times claiming he was disappointed in what he found.

The whole situation came to a head when Chester wrote a book in 1897 called *Twenty-one Battles Fought by Chester Bedell with Relations and Presbyterian Intolerance*. In the book Chester called his father-in-law "crazy" and went on to spell out his disdain for organized religion.

In a codicil to his will that he directed be published in the local newspaper, he warned his children to "Shun priests of all orders, doctors of all professions, and lawyers of all grades as you would a venomous serpent." Chester went on to claim, "Priests blunt the intellect and rob you of your learning. Doctors destroy your system to rob you of your earnings."

He went to the W. H. Mullins Company, a monument works in Salem, Ohio, and commissioned a life-size bronze statue of himself. The statue shows Chester, his foot on a scroll labeled "Superstition" and his hand holding a plaque that reads, "Universal Mental Liberty."

The capper came when he announced publicly, "If there is a God, let snakes infest my grave."

According to the legend, when Chester finally passed away in 1908, the people digging his grave in the Hartzell Cemetery near North Benton, Ohio, encountered several snakes. In addition, in the weeks, months, and years after his death, snakes were frequently found in and around his grave and monument. In fact, there were even occasions when snakes would be found, dead and alive, draped on Chester's monument, which towered over the grave.

Needless to say there were many people who believed that Chester got just what he asked for.

Word spread, and soon the little country cemetery was inundated by curious believers and nonbelievers trampling over other head-

Some said this statue was struck by lightening; others said a wind from the heavens blew it away.

stones to see the grave where the snakes crawled in and out of the ground. Even the famous evangelist Billy Sunday made a visit to the gravesite. People came in busloads. Chester, in death, had become a tourist attraction.

Religious tracts were published about the phenomenon. One even claimed that lightning had struck Chester's statue, toppling it to the ground. Another claimed a giant wind had torn the statue loose from its pedestal and smashed it into the earth below. Whatever happened, it was a fact that the statue was missing.

But Ivan Hoyle of the township's historical society says the facts are not quite so dramatic.

For openers, Chester's grave was on the bank of a river, and snakes were not uncommon along the riverbank. As for the snakes found on or around the statue, Hoyle blames those on teenagers and vandals who put them there for various reasons. And what about the story of the statue being destroyed by a lightning bolt or a great wind? Not true, says Hoyle. In fact, members of Chester's family took down the statue in the 1940s after vandals used Chester's bronze image as a target and pumped nineteen bullet holes into his head and body.

The bullet-riddled statue was stored in a family member's barn for many years; only in the last decade or so was it finally loaned to the Historical Society, where it is on display inside their museum. (The building has a sign on the front door saying that no firearms are permitted on the premises; seems they are taking no chances that someone might still want to take a shot at Chester.)

Was Chester Bedell an atheist? Hoyle says he has some doubts about that part of the legend too. He claims family members have told him that while Bedell would not say grace at the dinner table, he would always invite guests to pray. Also, the bell that still rings every Sunday in the Berlin Township Methodist Church was a gift from Chester Bedell.

One thing is for certain: Chester was not allowed to rest in peace. His original grave is now underwater. The construction of the Berlin Reservoir in 1941 created a lake where Chester's original grave was located, so the bodies of Chester and his family members were dug up and moved to higher ground near the front of the Hartzell Cemetery. When I visited the cemetery recently while researching this book, I noticed something interesting. While most of the tombstones face the lake, Chester's stone and those of his family are facing the opposite direction. Chester always did like to be a bit different.

The statue can be seen at the Berlin Township Historical Society, Berlin Township Hall, 15823 W. Akron-Canfield Road, Berlin, Ohio 44610. Hours vary.

The Bedell grave is located in Hartzell Cemetery in Deerfield Township, Portage County.

The President's Cemetery (That Isn't)

WOOSTER

There is a small cemetery in Wooster, Ohio, that many local folks refer to as "the president's cemetery." But not one U.S. president is buried here. So why the name?

Back in 1853 John and Elizabeth Plank of Wooster drew up a deed asking U.S. President Franklin Pierce to "hold the cemetery in trust for them and their heirs." Some people believe that the Planks, who presumably thought Wayne County, and Ohio in particular, was a fitting place for a presidential grave, were offering the cemetery to President Pierce and his family as a last resting place; others believe they wanted the president, and presumably those that came after him, to be a trustee and maintain the graves of the Plank family.

Whichever way it was, there is no record that President Pierce, who was probably preoccupied with running the country, ever considered using it or volunteered to take care of the plot for the Plank

There is still some confusion on just why this cemetery was offered to the president of the United States.

family. But you can see the original deed in the Wayne County historical records, and the cemetery is still located on Portage Road in downtown Wooster.

Warren Guthrie, Broadcasting Legend
CLEVELAND

It's no secret. When we see the television anchormen and women looking directly at us through the TV screen, we know they are reading their news scripts from a teleprompter, a unit hung on the camera that projects the script onto a screen in front of the camera lens that only the anchorperson can see. It allows them to look like they have memorized the script or, at best, are just having a nice conversation with us.

It wasn't always like this. In the early days of television, performers like Ohioan Bob Hope often joked about the man who held giant cards with the script, handwritten, in huge letters just off to the side of the camera, out of view. If you watch tapes of Hope's old shows and watch his eyes closely, you will note that he rarely looks directly at the camera; most often he is looking just beside it, reading the cue cards.

Sure, people could just ad-lib, but let's face it, anchorpersons aren't always knowledgeable about the topics they are reporting on. Even the president of the United States takes no chances when doing a formal speech. Those little glass wings you see on both sides of the podium are really the teleprompter with the president's speech on it.

Obviously there are situations where a teleprompter is not available or, because of lighting conditions, cannot be seen. Then some anchor folks rely on a device called an IFB, a little speaker that is plugged into their ear. Someone off camera reads the script to them, and they repeat it on camera looking just like they have it all memorized.

This looks easier than it really is. My colleague at Fox 8 TV, Tim Taylor, is one of the masters of this art; he can stand in the middle of a crowded, noisy room at a political convention and appear to have encyclopedic knowledge of the event and its upcoming schedule. He is able to smoothly and professionally do his report as though it were just born in his brain. You would never know that someone off camera, or perhaps hundreds of miles away, was feeding him the script through his earphone.

I, however, failed miserably on several occasions when I tried this. It was like trying to speak on a microphone in a large stadium, when your words echo back to you. But in reverse. One part of your brain tries to process the incoming words while another part of your brain tries to get your mouth to repeat the phrases. The end result was a collision someplace in my gray matter that caused total confusion. I would skip several sentences every few seconds so that what I do manage to repeat makes absolutely no sense to the person watching and listening.

In the early days of television, before teleprompters, another colleague of mine, anchorman Doug

Warren Guthrie did an entire newscast with no script, no teleprompter, and with just a few notes, night after night.

Adair from Xenia, Ohio, was blessed with a very good memory. He could look down at his script and memorize sentences at a glance. You would only occasionally see him glance down at his printed script. Once in a while he would forget a line, but since in those days anchormen had to write their own scripts, he usually was familiar with the material and could ad-lib a line or two until he found his place in the script.

But the man who became a real legend in Ohio television was a mild-mannered speech professor from Cleveland's Case Western Reserve University, Dr. Warren Guthrie. "Doc" Guthrie did a fifteen-minute sponsored news show over a state network of television stations, originating at WJW-TV in Cleveland. He did this five nights a week, without a teleprompter, without an IFB, without even a script. The entire newscast was usually written as a few lines of notes on three-by-five index cards.

Guthrie talked almost extemporaneously for about twelve to thirteen minutes each night, covering maybe fifteen to twenty different topics ranging from state news to national events (in those early days networks only had news shows in the early evening). There were few or no graphics or pictures, just Dr. Guthrie sitting at a desk, looking at the camera, and talking to you. Sometimes he would get up and walk to a globe to point out a remote area where some story was occurring.

I have interviewed staff members who worked with him at the time, and they claim that his shows always ended on time, never more than a few seconds off either way, an accomplishment almost unheard of in television.

In an interview shortly before his death in 1986, I asked him how he did it.

"I was blessed with a photographic mind," he told me, "We didn't have teleprompters or computers, and so I just had to remember everything."

He said he would write the topic of a story on a card and make a few notes about points he wanted to remind himself to make in the story, and then go on to the next subject. Usually he would spend the time just before his show reading the latest wire reports and making mental notes about other items he wanted to include in the program.

In those days, with only a few television stations on the air in each city in Ohio, his potential audience each evening was in the millions, but he told me, "I always tried to think I was just talking to my family and friends. I never thought about how many people were watching."

His show, sponsored by the oil giant Sohio, was called *Sohio Reporter* and was extremely popular for over twelve years, winning many awards.

In 1963 local television news was changing. "News teams" made up of anchormen, sportscasters, and weather people were gaining in popularity, and so WJW-TV replaced Guthrie with a program they called *City Camera News*. Sohio, in protest over Guthrie's firing, stopped their sponsorship of the news program. Guthrie for a brief time appeared on a local radio station, WHK, but finally left broadcasting to become director of public relations for Sohio, a job he held until his retirement in 1976.

Putting on a local television news show today takes the talents and work of reporters, writers, producers, assistant producers, news assignment editors, managing editors, graphics departments, and a host of other people, not to mention mini-cams and computers. In 1960 Warren Guthrie did it all by himself and became a television legend.

Chewing Gum

CLEVELAND

Back in 1880 there was this popcorn salesman in Cleveland. His name was William J. White. He was calling on a grocer, trying to sell him popcorn, when he learned the grocer was unhappy. The grocer's store had received a barrel of chicle instead of a barrel of nuts that he had ordered. He didn't want the chicle, and so he gave it to White, who was an inventive man. White took the barrel of chicle home and started to do some experiments.

There was already gum being sold on the market, but it was pretty tasteless stuff. The flavor, painted on the chicle, just didn't last. Chicle just wouldn't absorb it.

White discovered that if he put the flavoring in sugar first, the sugar would absorb the flavor and then he could coat the chicle. He had invented flavored gum.

Well, almost.

At about the same time there was this doctor, Edwin E. Beeman, born in LaGrange, in Lorain County, Ohio. The son of a doctor, he followed in his father's footsteps and also became a country doctor in Lorain and Erie Counties.

While working in Birmingham, in Erie County, he started experimenting with new cures and elixirs that he could prescribe for his patients. He called his little laboratory "the wormery." During his experiments he discovered that pepsin from the stomachs of freshly butchered hogs aided in human digestion. He created a powder out of this pepsin and started giving it to his patients. They loved it. Dr. Beeman moved to Cleveland and organized the Beeman Chemical Company. At first he bottled the pepsin in little blue bottles with the picture of a pig on the label. For some reason—maybe it was the pig—it didn't sell as well as he had expected.

Nellie Horton, a clerk in a stationery store, heard the good doctor complaining about business and made a suggestion to him. She was chewing some of the new Yucatan Chewing Gum invented by William J. White. Why not add some pepsin to chewing gum?

Dr. Beeman admitted that during his years of experimenting on new cures for his patients he had developed a chewing gum, but he said the stuff was like glue and tasted terrible.

Horton persisted and pointed out that pepsin had a nice flavor and if it worked he could probably sell a lot of pepsin gum.

Beeman made one of the better decisions of his life and decided to try it. Pepsin chewing gum was born. The only problem was that he still had a picture of a pig on the label with the motto, "With pepsin, you can eat like a pig." Sales were good, but not as good as they should have been. One of the first things his financiers did when organizing his new chewing gum company was to get rid of the pig and the motto. Instead they placed a picture of Dr. Beeman on the label. He was a balding man with a mustache and beard. Sales started to take off like a rocket, and Dr. Beeman became a very wealthy man.

Oh, remember Nellie Horton, who suggested the idea? He didn't forget her. According to some historians, Beeman gave her a block of stock in the new chewing gum company, and she also did well financially.

So the next time you put a wad of Juicy Fruit or Doublemint in your jaw, remember William J. White, Dr. Edwin Beeman, and Nellie Horton, who made gum taste good.

One Store, Two States

MASURY

The Penn-Ohio Medicine Mart is a most unusual pharmacy: it straddles the state line between Pennsylvania and Ohio. Part of the store is in one state and part of it is in another.

This means, for instance, that when they sell lottery tickets they have to have two machines, one for each state's lottery, and the machines have to be legally located in the state that issues the tickets. So what management has done is draw a line down through the store; as you shop, you cross back and forth from one state to the other—soft drinks in Ohio, prescriptions filled in Pennsylvania.

The store even has two mailing addresses: 830 South Irvine Avenue, Sharon, Pennsylvania, and 830 South Irvine Avenue, Masury, Ohio. The phone numbers are also different. If you are in Pennsylvania and you want to call the Penn-Ohio Medicine Mart, the number is 724-347-5505; Ohioans dial 330-448-0770.

When asked if dealing with laws in two states and having two addresses and phone numbers was confusing, a clerk just smiled and said, "You get used to it." But she said it does get hectic when one of the two state lotteries reaches an unusually high amount. "Then we have lines that literally spill from one state to the next."

The Penn-Ohio Medicine Mart, 830 South Irvine Avenue, Sharon, Pennsylvania, and Masury, Ohio, 330-448-0770 (Ohio) and 724-347-5505 (Pennsylvania), www. maxpages.com/paohmedmart

Cemetery Root Beer

CLEVELAND

Lake View Cemetery in Cleveland is famous as the final resting place of U.S. President James A. Garfield and a host of other famous Ohioans, from crime fighter Eliot Ness to professional baseball's only player killed by a pitched ball, Raymond Chapman.

But Lake View Cemetery now has another claim to fame: it has its own name-brand root beer for sale. That's right: cemetery visitors in Cleveland can refresh themselves with a cold bottle of Lake View Cemetery Root Beer. The drink comes in a period-style glass bottle with a picture of the cemetery's front gate on the label, but it has a modern twist-off cap.

And, are you ready for this? At certain times of the year you can buy not only a Lake View Cemetery Root Beer but also a hot dog with mustard, onions, and the works at the same cemetery where a former president of the United States is entombed.

No, the cemetery has not fallen on hard times. It's part of a marketing plan to make the cemetery more attractive to those who come here to visit. As I pointed out in an earlier book, *Ohio Oddities*, Lake View has long encouraged visitors to picnic on the cemetery grounds. They have even gone so far as to set up picnic tables and trash receptacles in various locations around the tombstones.

Lake View Root Beer, which is actually bottled in western New York, was the idea of staff member George Porter. According to a spokesperson for the cemetery, the idea is to make the cemetery a place for the living, as well as the dead. The root beer is available on their Heritage Day at the Cemetery in July and at other special events they hold during the year. Ms. Krohmer said if someone is really thirsting for a Lake View Cemetery Root Beer during other times of the year, they usually keep a few cold ones in the refrigerator at the main cemetery office.

The root beer and hot dog idea started with celebrations marking the one-hundredth anniversary of the cemetery; they are also offered during other special events in the cemetery that attract crowds. We assume this does not include funerals.

Lake View Cemetery, 12316 Euclid Avenue, Cleveland, Ohio 44106, 216-421-2665, www.lakeviewcemetery.com

Neil Armstrong Flew Here

WARREN

There is a monument to an airplane ride in Warren, Ohio. That's right, a ride.

In what is now a Kmart parking lot, there was an airport where Neil Armstrong, the first man to walk on the moon, took his very first airplane ride. The monument is a half-size model of the lunar landing module *Eagle* that Armstrong and fellow astronaut Buzz Aldrin used to land on the lunar surface.

Armstrong and his parents lived in the Warren, Ohio, area in the mid-1930s, and it was while living here that Neil Armstrong's lifelong love of flight started. A visit to the Cleveland National Air Races is said to have been his first exposure to airplanes, followed by a Sunday-morning flight with his father aboard a 1920s-era Ford Tri-Motor airplane, fondly known as the Tin Goose.

What is now the Kmart parking lot was the Warren Airways Airport in the 1930s.

The idea for the monument to an airplane ride was the inspiration of retired professional photographer Peter Perich of Warren. Shortly after Armstrong's moonwalk, Perich commissioned an artist to do a painting depicting Armstrong and his father in front of the Ford

History happened in Warren, Ohio, in what is now the parking lot of a Kmart and a McDonalds.

Tri-Motor at the Warren airport. The painting was donated to the Neil Armstrong Museum in Wapakoneta, Ohio. Then Perich decided that there should be a local reminder of Warren's connection to the moon flight, and so he started on a project that took more than thirty years and the cooperation of local manufacturers, schools, and other volunteers to finally bring to completion—the building of a half-size lunar landing module.

On October 30, 2003, Neil Armstrong came back to the place where it all started, a Kmart parking lot in Warren, Ohio, and posed for a picture beside the half-size replica of his *Eagle*.

www.firstflightlm.com

The Slingshot Car

YOUNGSTOWN

Why would a Ford Pinto have an eight-foot-tall slingshot sticking through its roof?

While we're at it, why would you take the cut-off ends of underground tanks, paint them in pastel colors, and place them on end like so many Teletubbies homes?

Or take furnace ductwork and coil it in huge spirals so it resembles a kind of giant yellow snake?

All for the sake of art, of course. But while you might expect this kind of display in a modern art gallery or museum, in this case it really stands out in front of a Youngstown, Ohio, industrial surplus business.

Owner Richard Rosenthal admits that he will buy almost anything if he thinks he can resell it. "But I also have a deep interest in art," he said, while strolling through his store, which he describes as "miles of aisles."

He has invited art students to decorate the inside of his business, and they have. The forklift truck resembles a monster pink ladybug; the bathrooms from floor to ceiling are a rainbow of colors.

"It's a perfect marriage," Rosenthal said, describing his industrial surplus business.

"People are always making something, or doing something, and

It's said that students used to use the slingshot that runs right through the roof of this car to shoot watermelons and pumpkins across the street.

there is something left over. We take that and recycle it and find a customer looking for a bargain."

So what about the Pinto with the slingshot through the roof?

Rosenthal laughs. "That started out as a senior art student's project at Youngstown University." It seems the artist called his work *Urban Hunter*, and originally the slingshot was equipped with some surgical rubber tubing that could hurl projectiles several hundred feet.

Rosenthal continued, "While it was in front of the university students were known to place things like watermelons and pumpkins in the slingshot at night and shoot them across Wick Avenue at a museum."

When Rosenthal acquired the sculpture he changed the surgical rubber to some old garden hose that had no elasticity and also had the bowling ball projectile bolted to the car, to make sure its shooting days were over.

"Even though it doesn't work, it still draws a lot of attention from passersby," he said.

The slingshot car of Youngstown, a sort-of-Ohio happening.

Star Supply Bargain Outlet, 875 Mahoning Avenue, Youngstown, Ohio, 330-746-2969, www.starsupplybargains.com

Of Castles and Coloring Books

LOUDONVILLE

We've all heard the expression "a man's home is his castle." Well, one Ohioan took that expression literally. And the story of how he came to build his own castle is as interesting as the fantastic structure itself.

Jim Landoll is a living example of the American dream.

Life was not always easy for Landoll, who was born in Norwalk, Ohio, in February 1940. When he was eight years old his father died, leaving his mother, Mary, a music teacher, to raise eight children: Jim and his five sisters and two brothers.

"I remember when I was a boy she would have our whole living room full of guitar students," Jim said.

When Jim was in the fifth grade Mary Landoll moved her family to Huron, where Jim graduated from Huron High School in the late 1950s. His mother had remarried, but with seven brothers and sisters, college was not an option for Jim. He went to work at the Lorain, Ohio, Ford assembly plant.

He started out on the assembly line. A quick learner, he could watch a procedure a couple of times and then do it himself. He caught the eye of the bosses and was transferred to the production control department, where he became a jack-of-all-trades filling in for workers in many different positions.

Then Uncle Sam intervened. It was 1963, and young American men were all subject to military service. Jim was drafted into the army and assigned to the famed 101st Airborne Division, headed to Germany.

"We worked hard while we were in Germany," Jim says. "When I had some time off, a three-day pass, I would travel around the country. I saw castles. A lot of castles."

Two years later, with the rank of sergeant, Jim finished his military service, returned home, and went back to Lorain's Ford assembly plant.

He continued to get promotions at Ford, but Jim began to get restless. "I always wanted to make something of myself," he said. "I wasn't exactly sure how I was going to do it, but I knew I wanted to do something different with my life."

When he was a youngster he loved to draw cartoons. He was good at it. He started thinking about children's coloring books. Perhaps he could do that.

So he left Ford and got a job with a printer in order to learn the printing business.

By day he worked at the printer; in the evenings and afternoons he would work at a makeshift desk in the uninsulated attic of his home, shivering while he made telephone calls to prospective customers for his children's coloring books.

During these years Jim Landoll had married and become the father of four children. But now the marriage was falling apart. It ended in divorce.

His problems at this low point in his life were compounded by the fact that he had attempted to save money by having his coloring books printed by an out-of-state printer. That Christmas the printer missed the delivery date, and Landoll, who was counting on a big holiday sale of his books, was nearly wiped out financially.

Jim decided he was going to have to be more in control if he was going to be a book publisher.

Although divorced, he was determined to support his kids. But big child-support payments meant he had little money left for himself and none for a business. His possessions included six dollars in cash, a bicycle, an old motor home, and a 1974 Corvette he had bought from his brother.

He had an idea.

He drove the motor home to Loudonville, Ohio, to Truax Printing. Landoll worked out a deal with owner John Truax: when the presses were not busy, Truax would allow Jim to use them to print his coloring books.

Truax also allowed him to park the motor home next to the printing shop. Thus started some very long days for Jim Landoll, who was working full time at his day job then sometimes working all night to do his own printing. "I often would see two sunrises before I went to sleep," he said. He was living in his unheated motor home. Sometimes his only food was canned soup.

"I remember the first big sale I made," Jim said. "It was 25,000 coloring books for the Eastgate Mall in Cincinnati, Ohio."

There was a catch: the deal called for him to deliver the books. He couldn't afford to ship them. The cost of gasoline to drive the motor home all the way across the state was way too much. That left only his old Corvette.

"I packed books in every inch of that car," he said, laughing. "I had them everywhere, on the floor, in the trunk, behind the seats and on the seats. I just left enough space for me to drive. I couldn't even see out of the right side of the car. I had books piled to the ceiling."

He made the delivery.

His business increased. He was finally able to afford an apartment, and he worked out a deal to operate a small printing company in nearby Hayesville, Ohio. To save money he started riding his bicycle from Loudonville to Hayesville, a thirty-two-mile round trip. But he was still working alone and would often go two complete days without sleep to be sure an order was completed on time.

In Hayesville he would go to a small restaurant, the Blue Willow, to eat each day, when he remembered to eat. He noticed the attractive young waitress but never really had a conversation with her, outside of ordering his food.

It was shortly before Memorial Day 1981. He was eating in the Blue Willow when the waitress, whose name was Marta, asked him if he had ever assembled a child's swing set.

Marta, it turned out, was divorced with a two-year-old daughter, Memory.

Jim allowed that he might be able to do it. He promised to stop over on Memorial Day and do the job.

Jim Landoll will never forget that Memorial Day. After the task was finished, he and Marta started talking. They talked for hours, well into the night. There was something very special about this woman. Jim suddenly decided to ask Marta to marry him.

She said, "I have to think about it."

He said, "I need to know now."

She waited until the next day when, over the objections of her relatives, she said yes, and they were married six weeks later. They have been married now for more than twenty-three years.

With Marta at his side, the coloring book business was starting to boom. They diversified, printing small books, Bibles, and even crossword puzzles. They were able to hire some help. They finally moved the operation to Mifflin, near Mansfield, Ohio, and a larger printing plant that had offices and storage.

By 1992 the business had started to be everything that Jim had dreamed of. They had more than two hundred employees, and Jim was starting to realize what success was, when his luck seemingly ran out.

He and Marta were at lunch near Mansfield when one of their employees ran into the restaurant screaming, "The factory in Mifflin is on fire!"

By the time Jim and Marta reached the scene all that was left of their business was a huge pile of ashes. They had lost nearly everything.

Even though they were insured, it was not enough to cover all the costs of starting again from scratch. Marta and other family members told Jim, "It's over." They might as well start trying to plan some new way to make a living.

Jim was insistent that they try again. He and Marta went to their bank to see about a loan to rebuild their plant, but the banker told them that statistics showed that most small businesses that suffered losses like the Landolls' usually did not survive.

Jim said, "At that point I fired the bank." It also steeled his determination to rebuild his business.

He was finally able to arrange for some of the money through other sources.

Then a friend, Larry Aber, called about a factory that was available in Ashland, Ohio. It was the old F. E. Meter Dump Company.

"I think every window in the place was knocked out," Jim recalled. "It had been heavily vandalized." But the price was right, and Aber even offered to throw in an old Lincoln limousine that had once belonged to the singing group Alabama.

The Landolls didn't really have any need for the limousine, but the offer intrigued them, and the reconstruction of their business began.

A Swiss company they had done business with called and offered them a printing press. Jim explained that they were in the midst of buying a building and didn't have funds to buy equipment yet. The Swiss company's executive said, "Don't worry about the money, your credit is good with us." The press arrived a few days later.

But there were still problems. Jim discovered some of their competitors had been contacting their customers and assuring them that the Landolls were out of business and would not be able to fulfill their orders.

Jim was determined to prove they were wrong. But they had no artwork; it had been destroyed. He, Marta, and their employees went on a mission to search their homes for copies of their books. They photocopied the books and were able to hire other printers to complete most of their unfulfilled orders.

In the meantime they continued to fix up the old factory and install their new equipment. "It wasn't the best way to print books," Jim says, "but it was acceptable and it kept us in business while we were recovering." By September of that year they were back to 80 percent of their capacity.

By the mid-1990s they had not only recovered much of their old business but had even surpassed their production before the fire. They now had more than 850 employees and were selling their products to major companies all over.

Jim Landoll had done something special with his life. He had succeeded. Landoll, Inc., had become the sixth-largest printer of children's books in the world.

That was when Jim bought a 73-acre hillside farm southeast of Loudonville. It was to be a getaway for him and Marta. Since serving in the army Jim had been fascinated with castles. He decided to see if he could build one on his farm.

"I didn't have any real plans, just this sketch I drew of a building with lots of turrets and towers. I just wanted to see if I could build a castle," Jim recalled. "Originally it was going to just be a sort of fancy barn to house my equipment and tractors."

Then, in 1997 the *Chicago Tribune* entered the picture. According to news stories at the time, the publishing giant paid Jim Landoll $100 million for his business. For the first time in his life Jim had enough money and time on his hands to do what he wanted to do. And there was the matter of that castle.

Over the years Jim had been buying land in and around the area of his farm in Loudonville. The farm had now stretched into an 1,100-acre estate that included pastures, valleys, hills, forests, and even blueberries.

Marta and Jim decided that they should share their beautiful Mohican-area property with everyone. Why not make the castle-like barn into a real castle that could be a one-of-a-kind hotel and resort?

And so Landoll's Mohican Castle was born.

What sprang up in 2001 on the hillside forest off Township Road 3352 was unlike most traditional castles. It was more reflective of the fairytale castles that inhabited Jim Landoll's coloring books. There were towers and turrets and hidden gardens with waterfalls instead of moats. Whenever possible, the trees on the site were not disturbed, so when the castle was finally finished it looked as though it had stood there for years.

Inside there are eleven suites, each finished with handmade furniture, imported Italian tile floors, and luxurious drapes and bedding. The flooring alone for each suite cost between $14,000 and $20,000. According to Jim Landoll, when you total up the cost of the furnishings, bedding,

The castle that Jim Landoll designed and built looked more like something in a fairy-tale or in one of his coloring books than the traditional idea of a castle.

draperies, and special equipment, like gas fireplaces and custom-made bathroom fixtures, plus little luxuries like heated tile floors so your feet don't get cold when you get out of the tub, "each of our suites cost as much as many homes do."

And there is more. Another building, an upscale restaurant called Legends at the Castle, has joined the castle. Another new building has just been constructed to handle wedding receptions and meetings. There is an indoor swimming pool with a grotto behind a waterfall. There is also the herd of Black Angus beef cattle that Jim raises, which provides much of the meat served at the restaurant. A greenhouse provides fresh vegetables, also used in the restaurant. There is a riding stable with horses available for trail rides, a blueberry farm on the property, and a sawmill. Jim even has his own emergency power system. When the eastern United States was hit with a massive power failure in 2003, his power system kicked in, and life went on as normal for guests at the Landolls' Mohican Castle.

Remember that Lincoln limousine once owned by the singing group Alabama? The one Jim had to buy along with that factory in Ashland? Well, he still has it, and now it looks just like new. He also still has the motor home he lived in when starting his printing business, as well as that bicycle he used to ride thirty-two miles to work each day. And he also has that '74 Corvette that carried his first big delivery to Cincinnati. What does he plan to do with them? He says perhaps one day he'll build a museum.

From coloring books to a real-life castle, Jim Landoll is living the American dream.

Landoll's Mohican Castle is located on Township Road 3352, in Loudonville, Ohio.

NORTHWEST OHIO

Two Graves for Anthony Wayne

TOLEDO

If you live anywhere in Ohio, the name of Anthony Wayne is a familiar one. There is Wayne County, Waynesburg, Waynesville, and Anthony Wayne Trail.

In real life Anthony Wayne was a soldier. He was known as "Mad Anthony" Wayne, and the things that happened to him after his death would be enough to make anyone mad. A monument to his most famous battle was erected in the wrong place. And what happened to his corpse is enough to inspire a Gothic horror tale. But let's go back to the beginning of the story.

According to Dr. David Frew, a historian from Erie, Pennsylvania, the Revolutionary War hero General "Mad Anthony" Wayne got his nickname because his ferocity in battle so frightened his opponents, usually American Indians, that they thought he was crazy and would sometimes run when they saw him advancing.

Despite all this, historians pretty much agree that Wayne, while a very competent officer serving under General George Washington in the Revolutionary War, did not stand out or bring notice on himself like others of Washington's officer corps.

It was the settlement of the Northwest Territory, which included Ohio, Michigan, and Indiana, that made him a hero and left his name on counties, towns, streets, and schools.

The 1783 Treaty of Paris, which effectively ended the Revolutionary War, had a little-known provision that let the British forces remain in the Northwest Territory at least until the newly formed United States was able to resolve disputes with the Indians over who owned the land. When negotiations failed, Washington (George, that is) used force and sent General Josiah Harmar to settle the issue. He was defeated by a confederation of tribes led by the Miami chieftain Michikinikwa, also known as Little Turtle.

The following year Washington sent his colleague General Arthur St. Clair and nearly the entire U.S. Army out to the Ohio frontier. His plan was to teach the Indians a lesson, get revenge for Harmar's defeat, and settle the disputes over land ownership. Washington also warned St. Clair to be prepared for surprise attacks, a warning St. Clair apparently ignored. He marched into a trap set by a much smaller Indian force, which nearly wiped out his command, and St. Clair had to run for his life. George Washington was embarrassed; the American army became a laughing stock.

Meanwhile the British, who were assisting the Indians in their battle with the United States, began to build forts in the territory with an eye toward annexing it to Canada. That was when Washington turned to Anthony Wayne. Wayne was given command of the decimated U.S. Army. He immediately started a recruiting drive, calling his new organization the Legion of the United States. He carefully trained the new troops and in 1794 was ready to march.

On August 20, 1794, he met the largest gathering of Indian tribes ever confronted by white Americans up to that time at a place just outside of present-day Toledo, Ohio. They clashed in a wooded area that had recently been ravaged by a tornado, leaving a tangle of downed trees and underbrush. The encounter became known as the Battle of Fallen Timbers. This time the training paid off. In a short fight, the Legion of the United States routed the Indians and sent them running back toward Detroit and the safety of the British forts. Wayne and his troops followed them along the Maumee River, destroying the Indians' villages and crops and forcing some who had lived along the river for hundreds of years to leave their homes. The Indians scurrying toward the British forts got another surprise. The British locked their gates and refused to let them in.

The British had a ticklish problem. They were under orders not to have a confrontation with the United States, since they had just signed the peace treaty and their sprawling empire had more pressing problems in other parts of the world. They were not prepared to resume the war with their breakaway colony.

The Indians, with no place to go and no help from their British allies, finally signed the Treaty of Greenville in 1795, opening up the Northwest Territory for settlement by the Americans. While the battle of Fallen Timbers is largely forgotten today, many historians rank it, along with the Battle of Lexington in the Revolutionary War and the Battle of Gettysburg in the Civil War, as one of the three most important turning points in American history. Had Wayne lost the battle, the map of the United States would be far different today.

"Mad Anthony" Wayne had become a bona fide American hero. His name was given to new villages, counties, and even highways in the Northwest Territory. Later, schools and universities would be named for him.

It would be many years before a section of the battlefield was set aside as a memorial to the encounter, as well as to both Wayne and the American Indians who fought there. The problem was that the passage of years had dimmed memories, and no one was quite sure just where the battle had occurred. They finally settled on a

The Indians gave General Wayne the title "Mad Anthony" because of his shouting and aggressive behavior during a battle. They thought he was crazy.

bluff overlooking the floodplain of the Maumee River, and here they erected their statues and monuments. For nearly seventy years it was assumed that the memorial was located where the battle had occurred.

However Professor Michael Pratt of Heidelberg College in Tiffin, Ohio, who was an anthropologist, had a feeling that the memorial was in the wrong place. He spent ten years researching the battle, reading old reports and eyewitness accounts, and finding old government records. Much of what he read convinced him all the more that a mistake had been made. Pratt got together a group of volunteers, and started an archaeological dig on a site where he believed the actual battle had happened. It was nearly a mile from the memorial.

It didn't take long for Pratt and his staff to hit pay dirt. Using computers, metal detectors, and even government satellites, they uncovered 320 battle-related artifacts that proved his theory was correct: the battlefield monuments had been built on the wrong location.

Since then, the Toledo Metroparks and the National Park Service have taken over the real battlefield, and it will be added to the existing memorial to create a new Battle of Fallen Timbers memorial that will now include the real site of the action.

As for Anthony Wayne, well, just as he was being acclaimed in every village and town on the frontier, he died.

In November 1796 George Washington had sent Wayne on a mission to Detroit to make sure the British were evacuating their forts and pulling back into Canada. Wayne had completed his mission and was returning to Philadelphia when he arrived by boat in Erie, Pennsylvania, on November 19. He didn't feel well. He was said to have a "severe fit of the gout." It must have been a very bad case, because over the next several weeks his condition worsened, and he finally died on December 15, in much pain, while sitting in a chair in the blockhouse at the fort guarding Erie's harbor. He was just 51 years old.

They followed his last request and buried him, wearing his uniform, in a plain wooden coffin at the foot of the flagpole in front of the blockhouse. The top of the casket had brass tacks that spelled out his initials, his age, and the year of his death.

Twelve years later, in 1808, bizarre events began to unfold.

Wayne's family back in Radnor, Pennsylvania, decided they wanted the general's body brought back for interment in their family burial plot in the local churchyard.

Wayne's son, Colonel Isaac Wayne, took off for Erie across primitive roads and trails driving a two-wheeled car called a sulky. When he got to Erie he asked Dr. J. C. Wallace, who had been his father's doctor, to handle the arrangements for digging up the body and preparing it for transport back to Radnor on his sulky. Isaac Wayne said he preferred to remember his father in life, instead of death, excused himself, and went off to his hotel.

Well, when Dr. Wallace and some volunteers opened the grave, they got a surprise. Instead of skeletal remains, they found a body that was still intact. Just one leg and foot had decomposed. The two-wheeled cart was far too small to accommodate the casket and the full, petrified body of the deceased General Wayne.

Dr. Wallace, wanting to accommodate Wayne's son in his intention of returning his father's body to Radnor, decided something had to be done. He went to his home and got a huge steel pot, the kind used for rendering lard when butchering pigs. He then ordered General Wayne's body cut into large chunks and placed in the pot, now filled with boiling water. After some time, he was able to separate flesh from bone, and then he placed the bones into a trunk, which fit neatly on the back of the two-wheeled cart.

It's said that when Colonel Isaac Wayne discovered what the doctor had done he was not happy; he said that had he known of the state of his father's body he would have rather left him buried in Erie. But, what was done was done, and so Isaac took the trunk with his father's bones and headed back to Radnor. In the meantime Dr. Wallace took the boiled flesh, the general's uniform, and even the knives he had used, put them back into the coffin, and reburied it next to the blockhouse. So today

Dr. J. C. Wallace used this large steel pot to boil the flesh off of "Mad Anthony" Wayne's body so that his son could fit his bones into a traveling box.

"Mad Anthony" Wayne has two graves. One in Erie, Pennsylvania, and another in a churchyard in Radnor, Pennsylvania.

By the way, if you visit the Erie Historical Society you can see the actual pot used in preparing Anthony Wayne's bones, as well as a lock of his hair taken by one of the women assisting the doctor at the time of the disinterment, as well as the chair he was sitting in when he died. The blockhouse is located on the east side of Erie near the veterans' home.

Erie Historical Society, 419 State Street, Erie, Pennsylvania 16501, 814-454-1813, www.eriecountyhistory.org

Fallen Timbers Battlefield Memorial, Metroparks of the Toledo Area, 5100 West Central Avenue, Toledo, Ohio 43615, 419-535-3057, www.metroparkstoledo.com

The Statue That Can't Find a Home
PUT-IN-BAY

You can't help but feel sorry for Oliver Hazard Perry. He's an authentic American hero, yet his statue can't seem to find a permanent home.

If it hadn't been for Ollie, we Americans who live in the Great Lakes area would probably be singing "O Canada" instead of "The Star-Spangled Banner." When Perry confronted the British fleet on Lake Erie in the War of 1812, Britain was a major world power, while the United States was just a ragtag collection of states that had broken away from the British Empire to create a new and untried nation. It was definitely a case of a major-league power versus a minor-league power, the United States.

So what happened? Some historians just say it was all luck, being at the right place at the right time. But like all battles, the most important issue is who wins, and in this case Perry was able to send General William Henry Harrison the message that has resounded down through the years, "We have met the enemy and they are ours." The tiny United States had handed the mighty British navy a rare defeat.

Congress met to issue a gold medal for Perry. In years to come, towns, schools, ships, and even children would be named in his honor. In Cleveland, Ohio, a group gathered to erect what was to be the first-ever state memorial to Perry and his victory. They raised a total of eight thousand dollars and contracted with sculptor William Walcutt of Cleveland to execute the statue.

On September 10, 1860, Walcutt and a host of veterans from the 1812 war gathered, along with Ohio officials, at the center of Cleveland's Public Square as the statue was unveiled. The twelve-foot-high pedestal was made of Rhode Island granite, from Perry's home state. On one side was a small statue of a sailor boy, bareheaded, and on the other side was a midshipman with his hat on. The main statue, eight feet high, showed Perry, bareheaded. It is carved of Parian marble, chosen for its purity and white color. The entire monument towered twenty-five feet over the crowd. Thirty thousand people were on hand that day, and it was said that the statue would be an enduring memorial to the bravery of Oliver Hazard Perry and his men.

The Perry Monument in its glory days, when it was located in the center of Cleveland's Public Square.

"Enduring" lasted just eighteen years. Because of increased need for roadway space in Public Square the city fathers uprooted Ollie and trucked him over to the southeast quadrant of the square. But just fourteen years later the veterans of another war, the Civil War, started making plans for a memorial to their conflict, and they thought the perfect place for the new Soldiers and Sailors Monument would be, you guessed it, the southeast quadrant of Public Square. Well, the next thing you know Oliver Hazard Perry's white statue was carried east down Euclid Avenue to the University Circle area and planted overlooking a small lake. Until 1913. That's when they decided to build the new Cleveland Museum of Art on the very spot that had been chosen to be the latest enduring home of the Perry statue. By this time it's a wonder some wag had not suggested the statue be recarved to show Perry carrying a suitcase or that wheels be put under the statue. So, Cleveland officials hustled Ollie off to a new location, this one in Gordon Park, along the edge of Lake Erie.

But with the passage of years and the repeated efforts to put the statue up, then take it down, move it, and put it back up again, the marble sculpture was starting to show a lot of wear. So members of an early settlers' group ponied up the funds to have two bronze replicas of the statue cast. One they sold to the state of Rhode Island, which apparently hadn't gotten around yet to putting a statue of Perry in their state building; the other was placed in Gordon Park. The original marble statue, now no longer needed, was given to the city of Perrysburg, Ohio, a community near Toledo that was named in Perry's honor.

The statue that has traveled over much of northern Ohio now stands on South Bass Island, in the shadow of the Perry Peace Memorial.

Problem was, by the time the marble statue reached Perrysburg the Great Depression was under way, and there just wasn't money to put it up. So it went into storage, and there it languished until 1937, when it was finally re-erected in its new hometown of Perrysburg. The statue at last seemed to have found permanence in this north-western Ohio town. Make that sixty years of permanence. By 1997 the old mariner's image was showing signs of serious deterioration, probably brought on by the Ohio winters as well as the many moves it had made. The Perrysburg city fathers decided the statue had to be replaced, so another bronze replica was made, and it was erected in place of the original statue. Which was then placed in storage, yet again.

Well, guess what? Oliver's statue has taken yet another trip, this time to an island in Lake Erie.

At the start of the twenty-first century, a visitor center was built at the base of the Perry Peace Memorial on South Bass Island in Lake Erie, where Perry had sailed to meet the British. The city of Perrysburg offered the old statue to the National Park Service, which opened the center in 2002, and that is where it stands today. Indoors, out of the weather.

Park rangers tell me the historic old statue now has a permanent home with them. I can almost hear the ghost of Oliver Hazard Perry saying, "Yeah. I've heard that one before."

Oh, I almost forgot, remember that replica of the statue that was built to replace the original in Cleveland's Gordon Park? Of course, they decided to move it. It now stands in Fort Huntington Park at West 3rd and Lakeside in Cleveland.

The original Perry Monument is now located inside the Visitor Center at the Perry's Victory and International Peace Memorial, Bay View Avenue, Put-in-Bay, Ohio 43456, 419-285-2184, www.nps.gov/pevi
The "new" bronze statue of Perry in Perrysburg is located near the corner of Louisiana and Front Streets, Perrysburg, Ohio, www.historicperrysburg.org

The Secret of Perry's Monument

PUT-IN-BAY

Visitors to South Bass Island in Lake Erie can't miss the Perry's Victory and International Peace Memorial. At 352 feet high, it stands taller than the Statue of Liberty in New York Harbor, and it can be seen from miles around.

From its open-air observation deck 317 feet above the lake water, you can see the shoreline of Canada on a clear day. You can also see the area west of the Lake Erie Islands where Commodore Oliver Hazard Perry took on the British Fleet with a small group of ships and handed them their first-ever defeat. His message to his commander, General William Henry Harrison—"We have met the enemy and they are ours"—is a mainstay in every American history book.

The memorial, which stands in the midst of twenty-five acres of manicured lawns, attracts nearly a quarter of a million visitors each year. It is maintained by the National Park Service, and rangers are on hand during the summer months to tell visitors the story of the Battle of Lake Erie and its importance to American history.

What many visitors don't usually notice is a small stone set in the floor of the rotunda, just inside the doorway. It reads:

Beneath this stone lie the remains of three American and three British officers killed in the Battle of Lake Erie, September 10, 1813.

If you scan the walls of the rotunda there are plaques engraved with the names of the sailors who took part in the battle, and here you will also find the names of the six men who are buried beneath this huge memorial.

The American officers were:

Lieutenant Joseph Brooks, Jr., USMC, on board the ship
   Lawrence
Midshipman Henry Laub, USN, on board the ship *Lawrence*
Midshipman John Clark, USN, on board the ship *Scorpion*

The British officers were:

Captain John Finnis of the ship *Queen Charlotte*
Lieutenant John Garland of the ship *Detroit*
Lieutenant James Garden of the ship *Queen Charlotte*

We know all of them died in the battle, but we don't know how they died, except for one of them, Lieutenant Joseph Brooks, Jr., the marine commander on board the *Lawrence*.

The son of a Revolutionary War veteran who went on to become governor of Massachusetts, Joseph Brooks, Jr., was commissioned a second lieutenant of marines in 1807. He commanded the detachment of marines on Commodore Perry's flagship, the *Lawrence*. When the battle started, the *Lawrence* came under heavy fire from the British and was badly damaged. With nearly half of his crew killed or wounded, Perry was on deck directing the fighting, and alongside him was Lieutenant Brooks. A cannonball fired by the British struck Brooks in the hip, shattering his leg. He fell beside Perry, who was unhurt. The pain was so intense that Brooks begged Perry to kill him to put him out of his misery. He was carried below decks into the wardroom that Dr. Usher Parsons had made into an impromptu hospital. He asked Dr. Usher how bad the wound was and whether he would survive. Usher, who admired the marine as an "accomplished gentleman and officer" told him the blunt truth that he only had hours left to live.

As the battle continued, at least three cannonballs pierced the wardroom, further injuring and killing men being worked on there. As he grew weaker, Lieutenant Brooks asked the doctor repeatedly how the battle was going, telling him he hoped that Commodore Perry would survive the fight.

After several hours of fighting, the *Lawrence* was so badly mauled that Perry decided to switch his flag to the *Niagara*. He took Dr. Parsons with him in a small boat to the new ship to continue the fight and, eventually, win the battle.

At four o'clock that afternoon Perry returned to the floating hulk that was all that was left of the *Lawrence*. On her bloody decks, with dead and wounded all around him, he accepted the British surrender. Below, Dr. Parsons found that Lieutenant Brooks had not been able to share in the historic moment when for the first time in history an entire British fleet had been defeated. Lieutenant Brooks was dead.

Most people think this landmark is a monument, but it is also a tomb.

Later that evening, on the orders of Commodore Perry, many of the dead were sewed into their hammocks and dropped into Lake Erie. The next morning the fleet returned to Put-in-Bay, and the bodies of Lieutenant Brooks and the two midshipmen, along with those of three British officers, were taken ashore and buried in a common grave at the lake's edge.

The gravesite eventually became part of what today is known as DeRivera Park, and in 1913, when construction began on the Perry's victory memorial tower, the bodies were exhumed and moved to the new memorial, where they rest today.

Perry's Victory and International Peace Memorial, Put-in-Bay, Ohio 43456, 419-285-2184, www.nps.gov/pevi

The World's Greatest Amateur Astronomer

DELPHOS

Les Peltier was a farm kid from Delphos, Ohio, who grew up along the Auglaize River fascinated by the world around him.

When he was just a child, his mother, one cold winter's night, pointed to the stars above and gave him the names of some of the constellations. It whetted his curiosity so much that the subject became a lifelong avocation.

Les picked strawberries in his father's strawberry patch to raise the eighteen dollars he needed to send away for a mail-order telescope. He had discovered the local library and books on astronomy.

Some might say that Les's interest in the stars became an obsession. He would spend hours, any night the sky was clear, standing in the darkened strawberry patch, scanning the skies, learning the geography of space.

From an old grindstone and a fence post he made a base for his small telescope, and on many long nights, with only the family cows to keep him company, he would sweep the skies. Les Peltier also recorded what he saw in a nightly journal. The names of stars that helped make up the Milky Way became as familiar as those of his Delphos neighbors.

He joined the American Association of Variable Star Observers (AAVSO), an amateur astronomy group, whose mission is to assist professional astronomers in chronicling the behavior of the variable stars. These are faint stars that suddenly, and without warning, get brighter and brighter and then just as suddenly go dim again. At that time all the reports from AAVSO went to Harvard University, where scientists took the data and tried to determine the reasons behind the light surges in the variable stars.

Some of the folks around Delphos thought Les was a little bit crazy—just a farm boy who had dropped out of high school. (During the First World War Les's brother was in the army, and the family needed Les to help run the farm. When the war ended, Les decided he would rather spend his time studying nature and the skies than go back to finish high school.) While he had some social life, by his own admission his happiest hours were the cold, long nights he spent searching the blanket of stars overhead, making notes on variable stars and charting meteors that raced through the nighttime sky.

It was his incessant note taking that brought Les his first reward. Night after night, week after week, year after year he sent in his reports on variable stars to Harvard University. His reports were so concise, so informative, that Harvard sent Les a letter thanking him for his diligence and offering to lend him a four-inch telescope they no longer needed.

Les decided he needed an observatory suitable for such an instrument, so he set out to build

In this primitive, homemade observatory, now located in John Bryan State Park near Yellow Springs, Ohio, one of America's most famous astronomers made his discoveries.

a small ten-by-fourteen-foot wooden building in the middle of the strawberry patch. Using a hand cutter, he trimmed lightweight steel sheets into pie-shaped sections to make his dome. Old roller skates were used to mount the dome so it could be turned 360 degrees.

For the next four years Les Peltier swept the skies each evening using his new, more powerful telescope, seeing things that he had missed with his first eighteen-dollar scope.

Something different happened on the night of November 13, 1925.

It was nearly 11 P.M. Les was making a final pan of the skies before calling it a night when he saw something. What it was, he wasn't sure, but it hadn't been there a few moments ago. It appeared to be a fuzzy, faraway object. He tried to focus on it by adjusting the telescope, but the object didn't change. The hair on the back of his neck started to stand on end. The realization hit home that what he was watching was characteristic of a comet, and yet no known comet was ever seen in that area of the sky.

He wanted to dash to the telephone and call Harvard University, but he had to be sure, so he forced himself to sit quietly for another hour. If it was still there, it was a comet.

The moments ticked by, each one of them seeming like hours. He had to stamp his feet and wave his arms to keep his circulation going in the cold November night.

Finally, at a quarter to midnight, he put his eye back to the telescope. Winking, pulsing back at him was a comet.

He dashed across the strawberry patch to his home and put in a long-distance call to Harvard University. While he waited, reality started setting in. There were thousands of professional astronomers in the world that night using much more powerful telescopes, some that cost millions of dollars; surely many of them had also discovered this new comet, and his sighting was probably hours too late. But at least he would have the satisfaction of being one of many who first saw it.

He was wrong. He was first to report the new comet. The high school dropout had beaten some of the best scientists in the world, using an old, hand-me-down four-inch telescope in a homemade observatory located in an Ohio strawberry patch. Leslie Peltier had scooped the world and discovered a new comet in the heavens. A comet now officially known as Comet Peltier.

But that's not the end of the story. In a career that spanned sixty-four years, Les Peltier went on to discover eleven more comets and two novae. He wrote four books, and his autobiography, *Starlight Nights: Adventures of a Stargazer*, won him the Ohio Author of the Year award in 1965. In 1947 Bowling Green State University awarded him an honorary doctorate, and in 1965 the mountain in California where the Ford Observatory stands was renamed Mount Peltier. Harvard University astronomer Dr. Harlow Shapley called Leslie Peltier "the world's greatest nonprofessional astronomer."

Not bad for a farm kid from Ohio.

Leslie C. Peltier died of a heart attack in 1980.

Comet Peltier will return on May 3, 2336.

Today, thanks to the Miami Valley Astronomical Society, visitors to their facility at John Bryan State Park near Yellow Springs can see an exact re-creation of Les Peltier's "merry-go-round" observatory and actually use some of the controls that were in the original when he discovered the last five comets of his career. Contact the society or check out their website for hours (www.mvas.org).

Memorial marker and tribute can be seen at the Delphos Public Library, 309 West 2nd Street, Delphos, Ohio 45833, 419-695-4015, www.delphos.lib.oh.us/pages/local.htm

German P.O.W.s in Ohio

PORT CLINTON

In the 1950s, while serving with the U.S. Marine Corps Reserve, I spent a weekend at Camp Perry, Ohio, a national guard base near the Lake Erie Islands. We were there to do our annual qualification with our weapons.

We were housed in some old, small tarpaper buildings near the center of the base. It was early November, and it was cold. The small heating stoves in the center of the tiny shacks barely kept us warm. There was no insulation, only the two-by-four framing with insulated board nailed to it from the outside.

As I was lying on my bunk, I studied the graffiti penciled on the two-by-fours, left over from visitors over the years. My eyes wandered to a beam over my head; there I saw a swastika, the symbol of Nazi Germany, penciled in with some apparently German words that I could not translate. I called my roommates' attention to the ceiling decoration, and we speculated on how it got there and who might have been responsible.

The next day following lunch I had some spare time and wandered over to the headquarters building at Camp Perry. I found a member of the national guard, described what I had found, and asked if he knew how it had gotten there, or why. He laughed and said, "We put you 'jarheads' in the old prison camp section."

"What prison camp?" I asked.

Much to my surprise he informed me that during World War II, Camp Perry had been used as a prisoner of war camp for both Italian and German prisoners captured in Europe.

By 1942 the number of Italians and Germans who had been captured by allied forces was becoming a problem. General Eisenhower and other Allied leaders didn't want large numbers of captured enemy soldiers just behind their lines, so pressure was put on the British government to allow captured Axis prisoners to be shipped to Britain for incarceration, removing them from the theater of war. The Brits, of course, wanted to share the wealth of prisoners with Canada and the United States.

After months and months of British pleading, America grudgingly

Many German POWs were glad to be in an American prison during WWII.

agreed to accept an initial shipment of fifty thousand German and Italian POWs.

Then came the campaign against German field marshal Rommel in North Africa, which brought thousands more German prisoners into the United States. By June 1945 there were nearly a half million Axis POWs being held in prison camps hastily constructed all over the United States.

Americans were treating the Axis prisoners with kid gloves, following the rules of the Geneva Convention to the letter, in hopes that the good treatment would ensure similar treatment for Allied prisoners being held by the Italians and Germans

Rumors started floating in September 1943 that Ohio's Camp Perry, then being used as a reception center for new draftees into the army, would be turned into a prisoner of war camp. On October 1, 1943, the government made the official announcement that Italian POWs would be interned at Camp Perry. It was also announced that they would be available to work in the tomato fields and farms of northwest Ohio to help alleviate the manpower shortage plaguing farms because of the war.

One Italian prisoner of war was more than happy to be imprisoned in Camp Perry. It turned out that his father was an American citizen living in nearby Dearborn, Michigan. When the soldier's mother had died in 1927, the father had left the boy in the care of relatives while he immigrated to the United States.

The war came along, and the boy was drafted into Mussolini's army and eventually captured by the Americans and sent to the United States. His father, meanwhile, was working in an American defense plant in Michigan. Prison camp officials arranged for the father to have a joyous reunion with his son.

Because of wartime security both the prisoner's name and that of his father were not allowed to be printed. Presumably, he was later released and returned to Italy.

By 1944 the manpower shortage in America, especially in the farm belt, was getting critical. Jamaican workers from the British-controlled islands had been imported, but they were too few. Farmers had discovered that many of the prisoners of war were just youngsters in their teens, and most were happy to be out of the war zone and in America. They had a good work ethic, and friendships sprang up between many of the farmers and their prisoner of war laborers. The farmers pleaded with the War Department to send them more prisoners of war.

Harald Schroeder broke a 50-year silence to talk about his experiences as a prisoner of the United States during WWII.

Starting in the spring of 1944, the makeup of the prison camp on Lake Erie began to change. German POWs started arriving. Many of the first ones were veterans of Rommel's African Corps. These were tough, veteran soldiers, and when some were sent out to help harvest the cherry crop in Waterville, near Toledo, they staged a sit-down strike, refusing to work. They were carted back to Camp Perry, where they were put on bread and water rations for two weeks. Another group of prisoners was taken back to the Waterville cherry orchard, and they helped finish picking the cherries.

While the American government tried to isolate the die-hard Nazis in the prisoner of war camps and move them to a central camp for hard-core prisoners, some managed to elude them. For the most part, the Germans at Camp Perry were enlisted men, many in their teens and early twenties, who seemed relieved to be away from the war in a peaceful surrounding. But not all. There were escapes. The *Port Clinton Herald* reported on May 25, 1945, that two German prisoners of war escaped from their work assignments at a manufacturing company in Fostoria. The two, Hans Henkel, age 18, and 20-year-old Heldmut Killian, could not speak English and were rounded up a few days later. They were pretty easy to spot, wearing blue denim clothes with a large *P* and *W* on the back.

The American government, hoping to create a new attitude in the captured Germans, offered them lessons in English and in how American democracy worked. Some were won over, and when the war was over and they had been repatriated to Germany, they even went so far as to return to the United States to apply for citizenship.

When World War II ended in August 1945 there was much rejoicing in the prisoner of war camps, especially at Camp Perry. The Germans thought they were finally going home. But it didn't happen quite the way they expected.

British, French, Russian, and American officials in Germany were not wild about a half million strong, healthy former German soldiers pouring back into their devastated country. The four powers that had won the war were struggling to help get the German infrastructure working again and to simply feed and clothe the Germans who had lost everything. The last thing they wanted was a half-million-man army, probably containing many of the former Nazis mixed back into the equation. Besides, France and Britain were asking for compensation from Germany for the damage and destruction that had been done to their countries. One of the ways they decided to get their compensation was to make the former German prisoners of war help rebuild those nations before they were sent home to Germany.

And that is what happened to many of them, which extended their prisoner status for not only months but years.

While researching this story, I interviewed a German who had been imprisoned in the United States during World War II.

Harald "Harry" Schroeder was conscripted into the German Luftwaffe and later transferred into the Wehrmacht, where he was captured in the D-day fighting in France. In his diary he says that of the 120 soldiers in his unit, only 18 survived the assault by American tanks and infantry. They surrendered, and he was eventually sent to a prisoner camp near Battle Creek, Michigan, much like Camp Perry in Ohio, where he says he was well treated and well fed. He was allowed to go swimming in Lake Michigan and was befriended by some of the farmers he worked with, who supplied him with cigarettes and called him "Harry." Schroeder sat out the remainder of World War II working on farms and in canning factories near the prisoner of war camp.

But when the war ended instead of being repatriated back to Germany, he was released by the Americans and given over to the French, who forced him to work in helping rebuild France. He worked on roads and in coalmines under brutal conditions for the next three years. He was not released to return to Germany until 1948, three years after the end of World War II, and when he did, his sister, Rosemary Schroeder, said he was a thin, worn-out man she could not recognize as her older brother who had gone off to war as a teenager years before.

Harald Schroeder says at that time he was very angry with the French and the Americans for not releasing him back to Germany. He will still not discuss the treatment he received at the hands of the French other than to say it was "inhuman."

Today Harald Schroeder is a retired engineer and lives near Frankfurt, Germany.

His sister, Rosemary, did come to America and became a citizen but has never convinced her brother to come back to the United States to visit her.

Today at Camp Perry the only evidence left of the prisoner of war camp are a few of the huts the prisoners lived in, now used by visitors to the NRA National Outdoor Rifle and Pistol Championships held there each summer.

The First Automobile Collision

OHIO CITY

The first recorded automobile accident happened in Van Wert County, Ohio. (Well, it really wasn't actually recorded, except later in a few history books, but it did happen there.)

It was all because of John W. Lambert, a resident of Ohio City who liked to tinker in his garage. It was 1891, and inventors around the world were trying to build a true "horseless carriage." Lambert, some historians claim, was the first to do so.

He opened the garage doors and came roaring out, smoke trailing, motor backfiring, into the street. Now, at the time streets were not like they are today. In fact they were just smoothed-over dirt. There were even a couple of old tree trunks in the road. This presented no problem for the horses and carriages, but to a motorcar without power steering, they did pose a bit of an obstacle. It's said that Lambert roared up and down the streets and around the tree trunks a few times, and then lost control of the vehicle. His car slid into a hitching rail, knocking it askew. Thus Lambert was the sole participant in the world's first traffic accident. History does not record whether the police cited Lambert, but probably not, since there were no laws about automobiles in those days.

The Man Who Built a Mountain
BOWLING GREEN

The northwest corner of Ohio is really flat. Kansas flat. One of the flattest spots in America. It was once a great swamp that early farmers reclaimed because of the rich earth. They created an area of the Buckeye State that could pass for the prairies of the West, with long vistas broken only by a barn or a farmhouse on the horizon or sometimes a row of trees.

So what do you do if you live in Ohio's northwest corner and your grandchildren say they'd like to go sledding in the winter? That's the situation Thomas Price of Bowling Green found himself in. But Price is a man who can move mountains, literally. His specialty is large earthmoving equipment. So he decided if his kids wanted to go sledding, they would have a hill to sled on. He marked off a space in back of his barn and started piling up dirt to build his own mountain.

It may not be the kind of mountain that most of us think of. This one is only forty or fifty feet high. But on the flat plain of northwest Ohio it can be seen for miles. It's probably the highest spot in several adjacent counties.

Did I mention that Price's hobby is reconstructing old military vehicles, like jeeps and mounted recoilless rifles? He also has perhaps the last working World War II amphibious tractor that was used by the Marines on their island-to-island sweep across the Pacific. Price,

What do you do if you have a hill-climbing Jeep but live in northwest Ohio where it's flat as a pancake? Why, you build your own mountain!

a former Marine, also found a rather personal use for his "mountain." He has a large collection of jeeps that were once used by the Marine Corps, and he entertains his guests by offering them a ride in one of these restored jeeps almost straight up the side of his manmade hill. "I have to make sure that I restored 'em the right way and that they can still do what they were meant to do," he said as he shifted into high gear and we went plunging skyward up a steep, rutted path to the crest of his personal mountain.

Sure enough, from up on top you can see the dust devils dancing across distant grain fields. You can even see the traffic snaking north and south on I-75. For a minute or so Tom Price is "king of the mountain," his very own mountain.

The jeep collection is not accessible to the public. The "mountain" can be seen from the highway at 13277 Klopfenstein Road, Bowling Green, Ohio 43402-9523

SOUTHWEST OHIO

Monument to a Pig

MIDDLETOWN

Perhaps one of the strangest monuments in Ohio is the statue to a pig. It's located near Middletown, Ohio, in a community that was formerly known as Blueball (but that's a story for another time).

While the statue still remains, it's pretty well hidden today, surrounded by trees and located almost in a resident's front yard. It used to be across from the Towne Mall shopping center, but because of construction it was moved. In fact, many newer residents here have never even seen the statue or heard its story.

This is how it happened.

The Shakers, a now-defunct religious order that had started out in the eastern United States, spread west at the turn of the nineteenth century. The first of the sect in this area was a group that decided to settle in Warren County, Ohio.

The Shakers, best remembered for the fine, simple furniture they built, also were expert farmers, and like most farmers of that time they used fast-growing hogs as their cash crop. But the nearest major market for the hogs was in the East, more than four hundred miles away. This was before railroads and highways, so this meant the hogs had to walk all four hundred miles to market and, hopefully, arrive there without losing much weight. The hog that could do all of this was a far cry from the round porkers we know today. A thin hog, almost a razorback, that really didn't pack much meat on his bones, was the staple of the farmers. These nearly wild animals could handle the long walk to market.

When talk of canals and railroads started to be heard in the Ohio country, the Shakers were farsighted enough to realize that when pigs could ride to market, whoever had the bigger hogs would make the most money.

A Shaker elder, David Darrow, knew of a breed of pig called the Big China back east, and he dispatched one of his flock to travel there and bring back a Big China boar and two sows to start a breeding program.

This may be the only statue in America dedicated to a pig—the Poland China Hog, who came neither from China nor Poland.

The program was successful, and by the mid-1800s the Shakers had developed a hog unlike any that had ever been seen in the world before. However, by that time the Shakers, who believed that their members should always be celibate, had started to die out for obvious reasons. Until this time they had maintained a local monopoly on the Big China hogs, and other farmers were envious. Finally, a farmer named Asher Asher, who had immigrated to America from Poland, went to the Shakers and convinced them to sell him two of their best brood sows and a boar.

It wasn't long before farmers in the Miami Valley were all raising the new breed of hog. Some called it the Big China; others referred to it as the Warren County Hog. But the name that seemed to stick honored the man who broke the Shaker monopoly on the new breed. Most everyone called it the Poland Hog.

By the 1860s the hog had spread across the country and was winning so many livestock shows that they decided to give it a class of its own. That called for the ancestry of the pig to be traced. The Swine Breeders of America were confused. They knew of the Shaker role in developing the Big China hog, but what was this reference to Poland? Had the hog been crossed with a European pig?

That was when they learned about Asher Asher, the former Polish farmer who had purchased the first of the big hogs from the Shakers. In the 1920s the Poland China Breeders Association decided to honor the event with a granite monument that took note of the first pedigree for a Poland China Hog, erecting what may have been the first statue to a pig in America.

So when you read of the enormous prices paid today for a grand champion Poland China Hog, remember it didn't come from Poland or China, it came from the Buckeye State.

The statue is now located at the intersection of Towne Boulevard and State Route 25, at the bottom of a hill near the fire station.

A Curse on Lebanon

LEBANON

The Shakers were a quiet religious group that liked to be left alone to live their lives and practice their faith as they saw fit. While slow to anger, these people, who live close to the earth, could retaliate in unusual ways when aroused.

A case in point: Lebanon, Ohio, in Warren County.

Back in the early 1800s Lebanon was a bustling little village with a newspaper, a main stop on the stagecoach runs. It was surrounded by some of the best farmland in Ohio. There was even talk of Lebanon growing into one of the biggest cities in Ohio. At least, certainly bigger than the nearby village of Dayton, which at the time had fewer residents than Lebanon.

Then came the arrival of the Shakers. Their strange customs of celibate marriage, speaking in tongues, and "shaking" during their religious services caused a lot of gossip in the farming community. But it was the Shakers' system of communal living that really created a schism between the religious sect and the community.

The Shakers together purchased more than four thousand acres of some of the best farmland just west of the community.

With their vast holdings and plentiful manpower to share the work and operate the farms, the Shakers could and did control markets, getting top price for their animals and grain. This didn't set well with the small farmers and businessmen who had to compete with them. Over the next eighteen years, mobs repeatedly invaded the Shaker community, destroying orchards and gardens and burning their buildings, hoping to frighten them into moving away. The motives behind the mob violence were complex. They involved family feuds, religious bigotry, unfounded rumors, and, in some cases, just plain jealousy. A newspaper in Lebanon, the *Western Star,* kept the pot boiling with scurrilous attacks on the Shakers.

The Shakers retaliated by staging a boycott of Lebanon and its business places. When that didn't stop the violence, they called on a higher power.

Since their earliest history Shakers had had a great belief in visions. In 1820 one of them told the others he received a heavenly message that they should put a curse on Lebanon and a blessing on the village of Dayton, where their religion had been welcomed with kindness from the other residents.

So two of the Shaker leaders, Richard McNemar and Francis Bedle, saddled up their horses and rode into Lebanon. As they rode up and down the streets of the village before startled onlookers, they doffed their large black hats, waved them at the crowd, and repeatedly proclaimed, "Woe upon all persecutors! Woe upon all persecutors!"

Now as curses go, this one seems pretty mild. No "We're going to strike you with lightning bolts" or "Rats and cicadas will infest your lands for seven years!" Just plain old "Woe on all persecutors."

Satisfied they had adequately cursed the little village, the two Shakers rode out of town leaving behind a bemused population.

Later that day, McNemar and Bedle appeared in tiny Dayton and, standing in their stirrups, dashed through the streets, again waving their hats, shouting, "Blessings on you! Blessings on you!"

So did the curse work?

Well, we can't ask the Shakers, who themselves died out for many reasons—chief among them the fact that they opposed sexual intercourse. Lebanon and Dayton are still with us. Is it only coincidence that Dayton, the smaller of the two communities in 1820, before being blessed by the Shakers, today has a population of nearly 200,000 people, while Lebanon has only about 11,000 residents?

When America's Big Voice Came from Ohio

WEST CHESTER

Back in 1972 when Kings Island Amusement Park first opened in southwest Ohio, I was assigned by the television station I worked for to take a look at our state's newest fun park.

As we were getting off I-71 at the Kings Mill exit, we noticed our gasoline gauge was bouncing on "empty," and so instead of turning toward the park we turned the opposite way looking for a service station. We drove a few miles and suddenly found ourselves alongside a field filled with monster broadcast towers. The area was fenced in, and there seemed to be a guard tower over the main building. It just didn't look like the normal broadcasting transmitter site.

A moment later we found a service station, and while the attendant was filling our car (that's right, there was a time when service stations had attendants who actually put the gasoline in your car, and even washed your windshields), I casually asked him about the place with all the antenna towers.

"Oh, that's a big government facility, called the Voice of America," he said. "They got transmitters so powerful that sometimes our wire fences start hummin', and we even get music from our chicken house roofs."

He wasn't just kidding; the Voice of America transmitters were some of the most powerful in the world, capable of sending a signal around the globe.

To put this in perspective, the largest commercial radio stations today send out a 50,000-watt signal. The Voice of America transmitters were capable of producing a signal of 500,000 to 600,00 watts—ten to twelve times stronger.

How the Voice of America wound up transmitting from what was once a cow pasture north of Cincinnati has a lot to do with a man named Powell Crosley, Jr., and a pioneering commercial radio station, WLW in Cincinnati.

Crosley, born in Cincinnati, was a man of many interests and many talents. He invented a car bearing his name, a diminutive vehicle that could be afforded by just about any family. The shelves that we enjoy in our refrigerators today were the result of his development of the Crosley Shelvadoor Refrigerator. He also invented an AM radio that bears his name, and he was the owner of radio station WLW in Cincinnati.

In the early 1930s Powell Crosley decided he wanted to own the most powerful radio station in the country. With the federal government's approval, his engineers built a transmitter in farm country in what is today West Chester, Ohio. The transmitter was capable of putting out 500,000 watts of power. It could hurl WLW's signal halfway around the world and certainly to most of North and South America.

There were a few problems, especially for people who lived near what was later called Bethany Station. Some folks with metal bridgework in their mouths started receiving WLW's radio programs. Others said it was difficult to sleep at night, since their bedsprings started talking. There were also the complaints from radio stations in other parts of the country charging that Crosley's radio-station signal was so powerful it was crowding their frequencies off the dial. Crosley was finally ordered to reduce the power back to 50,000 watts, its previous level. Then came World War II.

Germany was using powerful radio stations to send propaganda into parts of Europe, and the U.S. government wanted technology to counter it. Someone in government remembered Powell Crosley, Jr., and his "super radio station" in Butler County, Ohio.

On September 23, 1944, an announcer stepped in front of a microphone and said, "We will speak to you about America and the war. The news may be good, or it may be bad, but we will tell you the truth." It was the initial broadcast of the Voice of America.

When WWII ended, the cold war began, and the Voice of America took on a new role, telling the story of democracy to the world. At one time it broadcast to millions of listeners in thirty-two different languages.

While the first broadcasts were made from the Ohio transmitter, the actual studios soon moved to Washington, D.C., to be closer to the action. The huge transmitter was thought to be safe because it was buried so far into the Midwest, in the midst of some Ohio farmlands.

Bethany Station in Butler County continued to hurl the voices of freedom around the world for nearly fifty years. Then during some government cost-cutting in the mid-1990s, with communism on the decline, new technology on the horizon, and the birthing cries of the worldwide Internet, it was decided to close down the Ohio operation. In 1999 the government decommissioned the facility, and the land was divided, half going to the local community and the rest sold to developers.

Today all that remains of Bethany Station is the original transmitter building and the giant transmitters inside. The enormous antennas that painted the skies around the building are gone; instead soccer fields and parks now occupy the antenna sites.

A local group is trying to have the transmitter building turned into a museum to commemorate the time when, in tiny West Chester, Ohio, Americans spoke to the world and told them, "We will tell you the truth."

Voice of America Bethany Station, Voice of America Park, 8070 Tylersville Road, West Chester, Ohio.

A Mystery under Serpent Mound

PEEBLES

Serpent Mound, in Adams County, is known all over the world. It sprawls over nearly a quarter of a mile and resembles a large snake about to swallow something. Scientists still aren't sure just who built it, or why. Evidence found at the site suggests it may have been the work of the people of the Fort Ancient culture, but no one knows for sure. The best way to see the mound, which over the years has been worn down to just a mild hump in the earth, is from a nearby observation deck.

But an even a bigger mystery at Serpent Mound lay far under the ground.

Geologists discovered that Serpent Mound is located on the western edge of a four-mile-wide circle where the bedrock far below the earth's surface, usually smooth and uninterrupted, has been cracked and broken and moved around. Just what caused this anomaly had been debated ever since geologists first discovered it in the 1800s.

One group of scientists said it probably was caused by an earthquake or underground explosion of gases or water heated by molten rock deep within the earth. The problem is, they couldn't find any evidence of volcanic action or figure out why, if it was an earthquake, it was limited to such a small area.

The other school of thought suggested that it might have been the impact from a meteorite that smashed into the earth at that spot, leaving the crater. The four-mile circle of broken rock has three rings, one inside the other, much like the bull's-eye on a target, with the oldest broken rocks standing up in the center of the bull's-eye. Scientists say that is the typical signature of an impact crater. But the first investigation into the strange mix of rocks showed none of the meteorite debris that is usually left behind by such an event, and so the argument continued.

The mystery was finally solved in 1997. It's explanation centered on a something called a "planar deformation feature," or PDF for short. Geologists examining some earlier rock core samples discovered PDFs in a sample from the Serpent Mound area. A report from the Ohio Division of Geological Survey noted that "PDFs are only found in the fractured and deformed rocks adjacent to or within craters formed by the impact of a meteorite or comet."

The incident apparently happened 260 million years ago. Speculation is that an asteroid weighing about two billion pounds hit the earth in Adams County at about 15 miles per second, causing the four-mile-wide breakup in the earth and, at the time, probably making one really big hole.

Serpent Mound, 3850 State Route 73, Peebles, Ohio 45660, 937-587-2796 or 800-752-2757, www.ohiohistory.org/places/serpent/

The March King
CINCINNATI

If you ever played in a high school band, you're probably familiar with the Bennett Band Books, written by Harold Bennett. Or were they?

You may have also played compositions by such composers as Will

Huff, Al Hayes, Gus Beans, Ray Hall, Harry Hartley, or even Henrietta Hall. Yet you might be surprised to learn that all of these works were *not* written by those people. In fact, they were all written by just one person, a man named Henry Fillmore.

If you don't know the name, you may recognize some of the marches he has written: "Americans We," "Men of Ohio," or "Military Escort," the latter a march that John Philip Sousa told Fillmore that he wished he had written.

In his lifetime Henry Fillmore is credited with writing and arranging more than one thousand pieces of music. That averages out to almost two every month for the duration of his life.

Why didn't he write under his own name, though? That's where the tale gets a bit complicated.

Fillmore was born in 1881 in Cincinnati, Ohio. His father was part owner of the Fillmore Religious Music Publishing House. Fillmore showed an interest in music at an early age, and by the time he was in high school he could play piano, flute, violin, and guitar. He also became fascinated with the slide trombone, but his father, a devout religious man, believed the trombone to be "too evil for any righteous person to play." He based this on the fact that many street corner musicians used the trombone, and they were also known to imbibe "the demon rum."

Despite his father's feelings, Fillmore went on to study trombone under Charles Kohlman at the Cincinnati Conservatory of Music, where he also minored in composition. After graduating, he went to work for his father's publishing company.

The fact that the family business was religious music presented a problem for Fillmore, because he would rather write a heart-pounding march than the slow, sometimes dreary religious music of the day. So to avoid embarrassing his father, Fillmore used a pseudonym, "Will Huff," when he wanted to publish a march he had written entitled "Higham" (named after a line of brass instruments).

If that didn't upset his father, well, his next escapade must have surely sent the strict moralist running for the smelling salts. Fillmore created a family scandal when he fell in love with an exotic dancer, Mabel May Jones. His family objected. They should have known better. All their objections did was to convince Fillmore to marry Miss Jones, and the two of them ran away to join the Lemon Brothers'

Circus. During the years the two of them toured with the circus, he as bandleader, she as a dancer, he wrote the ragtime hit "Lassus Trombone."

A few years later, he reconciled with his family and apparently convinced his father that band music was not the devil's music, because when he reentered the music-publishing business he literally flooded the country with his band compositions. Now, because he was churning out so many of his own works, he decided to resort again to phony names so as not to saturate or "burn out" the market for his work. Thus, easy band pieces were signed by Harold Bennett; if the music was of medium difficulty to play, the author was Will Huff or Al Hayes; and for the more difficult band pieces he became Gus Beans, Ray Hall, Harry Hartley, or even the female Henrietta Hall.

Henry Fillmore died in 1956, but the spirit and the music of Fillmore and his alter egos still live on wherever there is a high school or college marching band.

The Father of Disposable Diapers

CINCINNATI

Cincinnati resident Victor Mills was a big-time executive of a major company when, in the 1950s, he was babysitting his baby granddaughter and had to change her soiled cloth diaper. "I just thought it was a mess," Mills was later quoted as saying in an interview in the *Cincinnati Enquirer*.

But Mills was not your ordinary grandfather. He was also a chemical engineer and headed up research teams for a major consumer products company.

The messy diaper was still on his mind when he returned to work a few days later, and he called together a group of researchers and told them he wanted to see what the possibility was of a diaper that was absorbent, prevented leaks, and, most important, didn't have to be washed—that could just be tossed away.

Now this was not the first time Victor Mills had come up with a new idea for a product. He also was on a team of researchers that discovered how to make potato chips that were all formed the same way and could be stacked in an airtight can. The process eventually led to the creation of one of America's favorite snack foods: Pringle's Potato Chips.

The diaper that his team came up with met his criteria, but it needed the acid test. Mills grabbed some of the new disposable diapers and took them along with his family on a trip to Maine. He said he changed his granddaughter's diapers on the tailgate of their station wagon, and of course the family didn't have to share the ride with a bag full of dirty diapers anymore, making for a much more pleasant journey.

In 1959 Rochester, New York, became the testing ground for the new disposable diapers, which had been called Tads, Solos, and Larks. None of the names seemed to stick, so when they were introduced to young mothers in Rochester, it was under a new name: Pampers. The rest, as they say, is history.

Procter and Gamble, the company Victor Mills worked for, had a new product that would soon create a $10 billion a year industry—all because one grandfather thought cloth diapers were "too messy."

(To be fair, it should be noted that a Connecticut housewife named Marion Donovan conceived of the idea for a paper disposable diaper a few years earlier than Mills and Proctor and Gamble. But she did not obtain a patent and was unable to interest manufacturers, so Mills is credited with the invention.)

Victor Mills died in 1997 at the age of 101. In his lifetime he had twenty-five patents registered in his name, but he will probably always be remembered best as the father of the disposable diaper.

The Real Blue Jacket

XENIA

Ohio is home to four major outdoor drama productions portraying pieces of our state's history. All of them are based on real people who lived in Ohio's frontier days.

Trumpet in the Land is the granddaddy of these, having been performed since 1969. It recounts the tragic story of the American massacre of more than ninety American Indian Christians, including women and children. The amphitheater where the drama is performed in New Philadelphia is located not far from where the awful event happened, in Gnadenhutton, Ohio.

Then there is *Tecumseh,* the story of the brilliant and charismatic Indian leader who was present at the birth of Ohio yet ended his life fighting on the side of the British. Its amphitheater in Chillicothe is not far from where Tecumseh was born.

The newest addition to the state historical dramas is *Johnny Appleseed,* performed in woods near Mansfield, where John Chapman actually planted some of his trees and helped early Ohio pioneers.

The fourth drama is *Blue Jacket.* It tells the legend of the fierce Shawnee war chief who nearly drove the early pioneers out of Ohio but was eventually forced to sign treaties that opened the future state to settlers. The story that unfolds on the stage is that Blue Jacket was actually a white man named Marmaduke van Sweringen, who had been captured, along with his younger brother, by the Shawnees during the American Revolution. The Shawnees reportedly agreed to release the brother if Marmaduke would agree to remain with them. He did, eventually becoming a Shawnee warrior who was held in such high regard that he became the principal war chief of the tribe.

From the opening scene where Death Rider, a lone Shawnee on a pale horse, rides up onto a hill overlooking the amphitheater stage as the sun sinks behind him, to the war cries of his fellow Shawnees and the roar of the settlers' cannons, to a heartrending final scene as Blue Jacket rides off into the night—and into history—the play is filled with action and excitement that captures the attention of the audience, young and old. The haunting musical score by composer Michael Rasbury helps bring to life the script, written by W. L. Mundell. It is truly an epic. Audiences have applauded the show for more than twenty years.

But is the story true?

The producers of the show say they really don't know.

While most everyone agrees that the Shawnee chieftain Blue Jacket really existed, he may or may not have really been a white man.

The show's producers say they have heard from both sides. Those who believe the legend point to the fact that Blue Jacket's descendents have both American Indian and white blood. But detractors say that doesn't prove anything, because Blue Jacket's first wife, and the mother of some of his children, was a white woman who had been captured by the Shawnees.

According to the Ohio Historical Society, there really was a man named Marmaduke van Sweringen. A family Bible says he was born in 1763, which means that it would have been possible for the Shawnees to capture him during the American Revolution. However, there is also evidence that Blue Jacket was born in the early 1740s, which would be almost twenty years before van Sweringen. Van Sweringen was also supposed to have been 17 years old when captured by the Shawnees. He certainly would have been adept in his native English at that age, yet many documents report that Blue Jacket did not understand or speak English and had to rely on interpreters for translation.

And there was this: Blue Jacket was first noted as an emerging leader of the Shawnees during fighting in 1774. Marmaduke van Sweringen would have only been 11 years old in 1774, and that was long before the Shawnees supposedly captured him.

And finally the claims that Blue Jacket was really Marmaduke van Sweringen did not start until nearly seventy years after Blue Jacket's death. Nowhere is there any mention by his contemporaries, made during his lifetime, that he may have been white.

The Historical Society summed it up this way: "There is no proof that the story of him being the lost Marmaduke van Sweringen is true. That seems to be [just] a romantic story."

However, there is no doubt that Blue Jacket was an effective Indian leader who left his mark on the history of this state.

Blue Jacket Outdoor Drama, First Frontier Inc., P.O. Box C, Xenia, Ohio 45385, 937-376-4318. The theater is located at 520 South Stringtown Road, Xenia, Ohio.

The Anti-Horse Thief Society

BENTONVILLE

I have always agreed with Groucho Marx: "I don't want to belong to any club that would have me as a member." But I gladly made an exception to that rule when I discovered a particularly unusual organization in southern Ohio: the Bentonville Anti-Horse Thief Society.

I do not own a horse, nor do I plan to buy one, so why would I want to belong to an organization like the Bentonville Anti-Horse Thief Society? It certainly seems exotic. After all, how many people can say they belong to an organization like this?

Actually, quite a few. The membership, worldwide, is now in the thousands.

Bentonville, in Adams County, is just a wide spot on State Route 41 with a handful of full-time residents. Eighty-nine-year-old Verna Naylor is the postmaster for the little town (the post office is located in her home).

Mrs. Naylor says Bentonville's unusual group got started back in 1853, before the Civil War. In the sparsely populated rural county, horses were the main means of transportation, and there were few law enforcement agencies. Theft of horses was a serious crime, and it was becoming a serious problem, so local folks decided to do something. They formed the Bentonville Anti-Horse Thief Society.

"They'd go out and find the stolen horses and hang the thieves," Mrs. Naylor said.

The society would assign members and a team captain to search for stolen horses. If a member refused to take part in the search, he was fined five dollars. The reward for finding a stolen horse and returning it to its owner was ten dollars, which was paid from the dues of the Anti-Horse Thief Society. It's assumed that the society also paid for the rope to hang the horse thieves.

Horse thieves, at least around Bentonville, apparently got the message. Mrs. Naylor said, "Lordy, I can't remember the last time we hung a horse thief around here."

The state of Ohio recognized the Bentonville Anti-Horse Thief Society in 1880, granting them a charter.

"We're pretty much just a fun organization today," Mrs. Naylor said.

Besides being postmaster of the town, she also serves as toastmaster for the Anti–Horse Thief Society.

"We allow anyone, anywhere, to be members today," she explained. Thousands of people from around the world have paid the one-dollar fee to become a member-for-life of the society.

"We have an annual banquet the last Saturday of April every year," Mrs. Naylor added. "It's not dress-up. We hold it over at the cafeteria at the Burning Heart Campground."

Almost anyone can be a member here . . . except a horse thief.

The Burning Heart Campground is a religious camp located within the community.

"It can hold 190 people, and we near filled it last year," she said.

In 1961 the community erected a monument to the Anti–Horse Thief Society on State Route 41. In 2003 a state historical marker honoring the society was also added to the little village

The Bentonville Anti–Horse Thief Society is now more than 150 years old and still going.

To become a lifetime member of the Bentonville Anti–Horse Thief Society, send a $1 donation to: Bentonville Anti–Horse Thief Society, c/o Verna Naylor, Bentonville, Ohio 45105.

The Town Where Everyone Is in Love
LOVELAND

In 1972 it occurred to Dr. Roland Boike, president of the chamber of commerce in Loveland, Ohio, that Valentine's Day was approaching. And with a name like Loveland, he realized that this town was just made for Valentine's Day.

Each year on Valentine's Day volunteers help the local post office handle the flood of mail seeking a Loveland postmark.

Now, the town didn't get its name because it was founded by a lot of lovestruck pioneers. It just happened that when the town was laid out in 1850 there were a store and a post office near the railroad tracks run by a man named James Loveland. As sometimes happened to crossroads community, an oft-used phrase ("leave the mailbags at Loveland's store") evolved into the name of the town. The name Loveland was officially adopted in 1863, and the town was incorporated as a village in 1878. Oddly, parts of the community were located in three counties: Hamilton, Clermont, and Warren. This still creates some interesting problems for local residents when it comes to getting various county permits and licenses.

But back to Dr. Boike and his idea.

Boike suggested that the chamber of commerce create a special heart-shaped Loveland postmark and through stories in the media encourage people postmark their valentines from the real Loveland. The chamber agreed to receive the mail at their office, stamp the Loveland seal onto the envelopes, and then cart them over to the U.S. post office to send them on their way.

Well, there are a lot of romantic people out there. The first year, hundreds of valentines were brought and sent to the Loveland chamber of commerce. In following years, with more and more publicity, a flood of valentines started coming in around the first of February. It was swamping the small staff in the chamber of commerce office, who had to hand stamp each of the incoming envelopes. A call went out for volunteers. In the last few years no fewer than three thousand valentines arrived at the chamber's office to be given the official stamp of Loveland.

And there is even more. As the years went by new events were added. Each year a Valentine Lady is nominated and selected to be the goodwill ambassador for Loveland and the chamber. Her duties include visiting nursing homes, schools, and businesses in the area. There is also a valentine card design contest, with the winning entry each year being sold at the chamber office and area businesses. In addition, there are poetry contests for children and adults and even a big communitywide annual Valentine's Day breakfast.

Who says we Ohioans aren't romantic?

Loveland Chamber of Commerce, 510 West Loveland Avenue, Loveland, Ohio 45140, 513-683-1544, www.lovelandchamber.org

The Mystery of the Hopewell Highway
CHILLICOTHE

The ancient people who once called Ohio home left behind no written record but left signs of an advanced civilization with their mound building, tools, and decorations. They may have left behind one other mysterious remnant: a long, wide, straight-as-an-arrow highway that stretches over sixty miles.

Researchers like Dr. Bradley Lepper of the Ohio Historical Society believe that the Hopewell people left a great road that runs between Newark and Chillicothe, Ohio.

What makes this almost unbelievable is that it would have had to be constructed nearly a thousand years before Columbus discovered America.

The Hopewell culture flourished in the Ohio area between 200 B.C. and 500 A.D.

Dr. Lepper has been examining old and new aerial photographs of the terrain between the two cities and says that there are traces of what appear to be walls along the edge of a nearly 150-foot-wide strip that runs straight across hills, valleys, forests, and even streams, from Newark, Ohio, home of the Great Circle Mound, to Chillicothe, which contains the Mound City Site of the Hopewell Culture National Park—a distance of nearly sixty miles.

This in an era when there was no earthmoving equipment, when most everything was done by hand, using baskets and rudimentary shovels and rakes.

And Lepper believes this may not be the only ancient road in Ohio.

He says there is a distinct possibility that the Hopewells, whose settlements have been found over much of the Midwest, were building great roadways between widely separated centers of social and religious activity centuries before the first Europeans started their exploration of the United States.

So the next time you drive along an interstate highway, remember the Hopewell people may have been here first.

The Poet from Dayton

DAYTON

They met when they were just boys, Orville and Paul. Orville was white; Paul was African American. Orville's father was a church official, and Paul's mother sometimes worked as a domestic for Orville's family in their Dayton home.

Perhaps the reason they got along so well as youngsters is that they both were bright, curious young men who wanted to know how things worked and why things were the way they were.

At Central High School in Dayton, Paul and Orville ended up in the same class. Paul was the only African American in the group. But, according to some of his letters, his classmates accepted him. He was named to the school debating society. He became president of the prestigious Philomathean Literary Society at the school. He loved words. He wrote that he once saw a poem by Henry Wadsworth Longfellow and, since he knew a man in Dayton by the name of Wadsworth, he thought it might be his writing. So, he borrowed the book and discovered the beauty of poetry and words. He also learned who the real Henry Wadsworth Longfellow was.

In his last years of high school, he first became assistant editor of the high school newspaper and then editor-in-chief. And he was elected senior class president.

Orville, on the other hand, didn't enjoy studying so much. He liked sports, especially the new fad of bicycling. He spent so much time on his bike that he became a champion cyclist. In his senior year he dropped out of high school to join his brother in starting a small printing company.

Orville, who loved to tinker, had built the printing press, and one night his friend Paul dropped into the print shop to have Orville print up a newspaper that the Wright brothers and Paul had just started called the *Dayton Tattler.*

While chatting with Orville, Paul scratched a poem on the wall of the print shop:

> *Orville Wright is out of sight*
> *In the printing business.*
> *No other mind is half so bright*
> *As his'n is.*

Orville Wright was, of course, one half of the Wright brothers. He and his brother, Wilbur, would go on to teach the world to fly with their invention of the first prac-tical airplane that flew under its own power. Orville would be the man to make that first flight.

In 1938 Paul Laurence Dunbar's home became the first state memorial ever dedicated to an African American.

Paul would also find fame and would become a legend in the liter-ary world. He was Paul Laurence Dunbar, America's poet.

The *Dayton Tattler* eventually failed. But Paul and Orville would see each other again and again, even as their destinies led them on different paths. Their friendship would continue the rest of their lives.

> *I like to hear of wealth and gold,*
> *And El Doradoes in their glory;*
> *I like for silks and satins bold*
> *To sweep and rustle through a story.*
> *The nightingale is sweet of song;*
> *The rare exotic smells divinely;*
> *And knightly men who stride along,*
> *The role heroic carry finely.*
> *But then, upon the other hand,*
> *Our minds have got a way of running*

To things that aren't quite so grand,
Which, maybe, we are best in shunning.
For some of us still like to see
The poor man in his dwelling narrow,
The hollyhock, the bumblebee,
The meadow lark, and chirping sparrow.
We like the man who soars and sings
With high and lofty inspiration;
But he who sings of common things
Shall always share our admiration.
　　　　　　　　　—"Common Things"

Two years out of Central High School, Paul Laurence Dunbar managed to scrape enough money together to have his first collection of poetry published. *Oak and Ivy* caught the attention of famed Hoosier poet James Whitcomb Riley, who wrote to Dunbar and praised his work.

Praise for his talent was one thing, but making a living was something else. Dunbar still lived in a racist society, and despite his literary skills he was unable to find any job other than janitor or elevator operator. So by day he ran an elevator, and at night he toiled late into the evening writing his poetry, pouring out his heart and soul in his work.

I know what the caged bird feels, alas!
When the sun is bright on the upland slopes;
When the wind stirs soft through the springing grass,
And the river flows like a stream of glass;
When the first bird sings and the first bud opes,
And the faint perfume from its chalice steals—
I know what the caged bird feels!
I know why the caged bird beats his wing
Till its blood is red on the cruel bars;
For he must fly back to his perch and cling
When he fain would be on the bough a-swing;
And a pain still throbs in the old, old scars
And they pulse again with a keener sting—
I know why he beats his wing!

I know why the caged bird sings, ah me,
When his wing is bruised and his bosom sore,—
When he beats his bars and he would be free;
It is not a carol of joy or glee,
But a prayer that he sends from his heart's deep core,
But a plea, that upward to Heaven he flings—
I know why the caged bird sings.

—"Sympathy"

In 1893 Dunbar was given the opportunity to do a public reading of his poetry at the World's Fair, the Columbian Exposition in Chicago. There he met the great Frederick Douglass, who was much impressed by the young man from Ohio. But despite the praises of men like Riley and Douglass, Dunbar still could not get any nationwide attention of his work.

In 1895, with help from some friends, he published a second book of poems, *Majors and Minors*. A friend sent a copy to the "dean" of nineteenth-century American literature, the famous critic William Dean Howells. Howells not only liked what he read, he wrote a wonderful review of the work in the nationally published *Harper's Weekly*, a very influential publication. It finally brought Dunbar the recognition he sought.

A New York publishing house combined Dunbar's two books into a new collection, Lyrics of a Lowly Life. William Dean Howells even wrote the foreword to the new book. The collection has been cited as perhaps the bestselling work of poetry by an African American writer. Now, Dunbar was on the fast track to fame. He had become a national literary figure almost overnight.

A correspondence with African American poet and educator Alice Ruth Moore blossomed into a romance. When Dunbar returned from an appearance in England in 1897, they were married. Dunbar accepted a job at the Library of Congress in Washington, D.C.

But Dunbar had tuberculosis, and within a year he was forced to quit his job. He was supposed to rest but spent most of his time still writing and giving recitals of his poetry.

His health was getting worse. One of his recitals was in his hometown of Dayton, Ohio. A huge crowd had gathered to hear him, including his old friend Orville Wright and Wright's sister Katherine.

But Dunbar became so ill he was unable to appear and had to cancel the reading.

His marriage had fallen apart. He and Alice separated, and he moved back to Dayton where his mother, Matilda, took care of him and watched as he struggled to continue writing in the tiny study she had prepared for him.

Over the years he had written a dozen books of poetry, four books of short stories, five novels, and a play. He had been able to buy the house in Dayton where his mother lived. He was lauded all over the country, but he was not a wealthy man. Alcoholism and tuberculosis were draining his strength and his funds. Just three years after his friend Orville Wright freed humankind of its earthly bonds with man's first flight, the spirit of Paul Laurence Dunbar also took flight, and he died in his mother's arms. He was just 33 years old.

The racism he faced most of his life was subtly reflected in one of his most famous poems, "We Wear the Mask":

We wear the mask that grins and lies,
It hides our cheeks and shades our eyes—
This debt we pay to human guile;
With torn and bleeding hearts we smile
And mouth with myriad subtleties,
Why should the world be over-wise,
In counting all our tears and sighs?
Nay, let them only see us, while
We wear the mask.
We smile, but oh great Christ, our cries
To Thee from tortured souls arise
We sing, but oh the clay is vile
Beneath our feet, and long the mile,
But let the world dream otherwise,
We wear the mask!

After Dunbar's death, his mother, Matilda, kept the home just as he had left it. Visitors came from all over the country to see where he had created his works. When Matilda died, the state of Ohio purchased the home, and in 1938 it became the first state memorial ever created to honor an African American.

Sadly, the poem Dunbar was working on at the time of his death has been lost. His mother, in an effort to share his work with his fans, had left the poem on his desk where everyone could see it. When she died and the state took over the home, it was discovered that the sun had eventually bleached the ink, and the poem had disappeared.

The home on North Paul Laurence Dunbar Street in Dayton has been declared a national landmark. In 1975 the U.S. Postal Service issued a commemorative stamp in Dunbar's honor. Schools and other public buildings around the country have been named for him. His tombstone in Woodland Cemetery in Dayton is not far from that of friend and classmate Orville Wright. On the stone is chiseled a poem Dunbar wrote in dialect as a tribute to the songs and stories passed down to him by his mother and father, who were once slaves. It is called "The Death Song":

Lay me down beneaf de willers in de grass,
Wha de branch'll go a-singin' as it pass.
An' w'en I's a-layin' low,
I kin hyeah it as it go
Singin', "Sleep, my honey, tek yo' res at las'.

The Paul Laurence Dunbar Home is at 219 North Paul Laurence Dunbar Street, Dayton, Ohio 45401, 800-860-0148.

Sincerely, Woodrow Wilson

CHILLICOTHE

In 1918, just as World War I was winding down, two men came to Camp Sherman in Chillicothe with an unusual request. Arthur Mole and his partner, John Thomas, of Zion, Illinois, wanted to create a living work of art.

Somehow the partners convinced the camp commander to allow them to line up 21,000 officers and enlisted men. Then, using megaphones, they directed the men into a 700-foot-long design.

Their scheme took a week of planning and many rehearsals. All came together one morning, out on the parade field. Mole scurried up a 70-foot-tall observation tower with his 11x14-view camera strapped to the top. With Thomas on the ground, relaying his shouted last-minute instructions, Mole finally shouted "Cheese" or something like that and pressed the camera's shutter. The result? A surprisingly lifelike portrait of the austere U.S. President Woodrow Wilson.

Many a soldier bought a copy as a souvenir of his days at Camp Sherman.

A living portrait of President Woodrow Wilson created by arranging 21,000 soldiers at Camp Sherman, Ohio, in 1918.

Disaster at Chillicothe

CHILLICOTHE

If you had to pick a spot that best typifies the scenery of Ohio, it would have to be Ross County in the southern part of the state.

The plains and hills of Ross County have also been home to much Ohio history.

It is Mount Logan, east of Adena and home to one of the fathers of Ohio statehood, Thomas Worthington, that is pictured on the Great Seal of Ohio.

It was near here that the Indian leader Tecumseh was born.

But even long before these events, there was a civilization living in the hills and valleys of what is today Ross County.

First came the nomadic early Americans, followed by the Adena, the Fort Ancient, and then the Hopewell cultures; all of them left the scene well before European settlers reached the Ohio country. The Adenas and the Hopewells left behind them mysterious mounds, some used as community graves, others possibly for religious purposes or for some kind of astrological calendar.

A veritable city of these prehistoric mounds was left behind in what was to become the county seat of Ross County, the town of Chillicothe.

The name Chillicothe came from the last American Indians to live in the area, the Shawnees. They called it "Chalagwatha," which means town or gathering place. Chillicothe became Ohio's first capital.

Early European American settlers poked and probed at some of the mounds but for the most part just considered them a nuisance and, using plows, tried to smooth out the fields where they stood.

During the War of 1812, the 19th U.S. Regiment of Infantry was stationed in the then state capital at a place near the mounds called "Camp Bull." It was turned into a prison camp when Oliver Hazard Perry handed the British defeat in the historic Battle of Lake Erie. Three hundred British seamen, captured in the battle, were marched to Chillicothe and imprisoned for ten months. Before they were released, they witnessed the firing-squad execution of six American soldiers who had been found guilty of desertion.

During the American Civil War the site again became a training ground for soldiers, as the 73rd Regiment was formed and trained at Chillicothe before marching off to the war.

But it was World War I that brought the biggest change—and disaster—to Ross County, in 1917.

The wartime drafting of men to quickly field an army meant new training facilities had to be built. The relatively flat area of Ross County, with lots of available land, plentiful water supply, and nearby rail lines, made it very attractive to Washington officials, who on June 8, 1917, announced that an army-training center would be built at Chillicothe.

On June 28 the first delegation of army engineers arrived to start construction. They, along with five thousand civilian construction workers and their equipment, literally erected a small city in the next ninety days. It would become the third-largest army-training center in the United States at that time.

By the end of September, when the first soldiers stared arriving, they had built over two thousand buildings and barracks to house the doughboys.

At the start of construction the population of Chillicothe was a modest sixteen thousand; by the time the new camp, named Camp Sherman in honor of Ohio Civil War general William Tecumseh Sherman, was operating at full steam, the population of Chillicothe had swelled to sixty thousand.

There were problems. The city power plant had agreed to provide electricity for the new army base, but the city had not anticipated how big the camp would become. They found their 1,000-kilowatt plant straining to supply the 1,700 kilowatts needed. The city threatened to cut off the army's electricity so they could continue to light the town's streets at night. The army responded by marching armed soldiers into the power plant, seizing it, and turning off the street lights until new lines could be run to bring power from northern cities to the town.

At any given time, forty thousand soldiers were being trained at Camp Sherman before being sent overseas to join the war. But many would lose their lives in Chillicothe without ever hearing a shot fired in anger.

The worldwide outbreak of Spanish influenza, which would reach epidemic proportions in October 1918, reached Camp Sherman in

September. More than fourteen hundred cases of the flu had been reported at the base hospital, and seven people, including one nurse, had died as a result. But this was only the beginning of what became a massive tragedy.

By October the number of cases was swelling each day; the hospitals were packed with flu victims. Makeshift wards in tents and other buildings were pressed into use. The number of ill soldiers topped one thousand in the first few days of the month, and then two thousand, and it increased by the hour. The camp medical facilities were swamped. Medical officials declared the camp off limits to any outsiders in an attempt to quarantine the disease. But the soldiers continued to sicken and die. In that month alone there were more than 5,600 cases of the disease treated at Camp Sherman, and, sadly, 1,200 soldiers in that one month died from influenza.

The army had to turn Chillicothe's Majestic Theater into a temporary morgue. According to one historian, bodies were "stacked like cordwood." The alley behind the theater became known as Blood Alley. Almost daily, wagonloads of caskets were hauled through the silent streets of the town to the local train station to ship the dead soldiers home. Soldiers like Private Howard Primett of Lakewood, Ohio: he had only been a soldier for forty-three days when he was stricken and died.

The post band would accompany the caskets, playing funeral dirges all the way to the railroad station, and then, on orders of their commanders, after they had dropped off the bodies at the station, they would play lively marches all the way back to the base to try to cheer up the local townspeople and distract them from the tragedy they were witnessing.

Parents and friends of the soldiers flooded the camp with telegrams and phone calls suggesting cures for the flu. The suggestions ranged from having ill soldiers sleep over a shotgun so the "fine steel of the gun could draw out the fever" to making them "sweat for one and one half hours, or stand outside naked." One lady suggested that those who were ill would benefit from inhaling the vapors of a pepper stew. But in an age of few high-tech medical treatments, about all the doctors could really do was prescribe bed rest and hope the person was strong enough to survive the disease.

In addition to the camp, the town had been ordered quarantined by health officials. All public meeting places, theaters, and bars were ordered closed. The epidemic also hit Chillicothe, but the death toll was much smaller than on the crowded army post.

The epidemic and the war ended at almost the same time, November 1918. Within a year, the last soldier was discharged and gone from Camp Sherman.

Then the government wasn't sure what to do with the land.

Part of it became a veterans' training center, and the hospital was expanded into a veteran's hospital facility. Another part of the camp-grounds eventually became a state prison. There was even talk of using the rest of the land for another military training site.

Had it not been for the concern of a local man, a second sort of tragedy might have happened: the eradication of a priceless bit of American history.

His name was Albert C. Spetnagel. He was an amateur archeologist from Chillicothe, and he had become alarmed, back when the army first started building Camp Sherman, at the Army's lack of concern for the historic value of the local "Mound City."

Spetnagel appealed to state historical society officials, who were finally able to convince the army at least to turn one planned barracks sideways in order to save one of the larger mounds. But the army told the archeologists they would have to run some lines and pipes through the existing mounds. They agreed that care would be used to preserve any specimens, and that any unearthed would be turned over to the historical society.

The prehistoric mounds that made up Mound City had already been pretty well obliterated. Early farmers had leveled many of them and plowed over the earth to plant crops. Then the army nearly completed the destruction with the building of the training base.

Thanks to the efforts of Spetnagel and the state historical society, army engineers were instructed to draw diagrams of where all the mounds had been before the start of construction, but these were later found to be inaccurate.

After the war the government was pondering what to do with the abandoned base. In 1920 the Ohio State Archeological and Historical Society started excavating the site of the now empty Camp Sherman and found four of the mounds half-covered by barracks.

Local service clubs, headed by Albert Spetnagel, bombarded the president of the United States, who at that time happened to be Marion, Ohio's Warren G. Harding, with letters urging him to declare the mounds as "Mound City Group National Monument."

On March 2, 1923, President Harding signed a proclamation establishing the national monument. It proved to be just in time to allow the preservation committee to stop overzealous army work crews who were taking down what was left of Camp Sherman and inadvertently also leveling out recently excavated mound sites. Mound City, or at least what was left of it, was finally saved. The area would be preserved for future generations to study.

Today it is called "The Mound City Group of the Hopewell Culture National Historical Park." The Ohio Historical Society originally operated it, but in 1946 the National Park Service took over and continues to oversee the site.

Some of the mounds have been carefully replicated on the original locations, but we will probably never see the mounds as they originally were. Some had earthen walls twelve feet high and were over a thousand feet across. While researchers have discovered much about the Hopewell Culture, the mounds of Ohio still hold many secrets.

Hopewell Culture National Historical Park, 16062 State Route 104, Chillicothe, Ohio, 45601, 740-774-1126.

A Funeral Home Museum

WEST UNION

If you are interested in really strange museums and collections, this one might be for you. The William Lafferty Memorial Funeral and Carriage Collection contains not only old horse-drawn hearses from the nineteenth century but also a collection of the various tools that undertakers have used over the last hundred years or so. Things like burial clothing, shrouds, even old wooden caskets and embalming kits.

The collection was started years ago by William Lafferty, who operated a funeral home in West Union, Ohio. He began with a horse-drawn hearse he had once used in the family business. Then he started going to carriage auctions and buying more ornate funeral buggies. For years the collection was scattered in several garages and outbuildings, until finally, after Lafferty's death, his wife, Grace, together with his son John Lafferty and John's wife, Elaine, decided to construct a building to display all of the late William Lafferty's collection. The result is a collection of nine carriages and hundreds of other items, such as early funeral-home ledgers and even handwritten instructions from some of his customers for the disposition of their remains.

William Lafferty Memorial Funeral and Carriage Collection, 205 Cherry Street, West Union, Ohio, 937-544-2121.

Mr. Tingle's Gift

LEBANON

In the early 1900s communities in many parts of the country began to receive unexpected charitable gifts in the name of Jedidiah Tingle. The donations, such as money for playgrounds, were usually to benefit children, and they were much appreciated. But no one seemed to know just who Jedidiah Tingle was or where he was from. There was one clue. Some of the gifts also contained a photo of a tombstone.

We're not talking about an isolated incident here; donations were made to 119 communities in more than 32 states, totaling thousands of dollars. It was enough to raise the curiosity of the *New York Times*, which put a reporter to work finding out who the mysterious Jedidiah Tingle was and why was he being so charitable.

It turned out that Jedidiah Tingle was a dead man. He had died in Lebanon, Ohio, on April 2, 1827, nearly a hundred years before his gifts started arriving in communities all over America. The reporter then discovered that the man who had been signing Jedidiah Tingle's name to the gifts was in fact William Elmer Harmon, also from Lebanon, Ohio, and the great-grandson of Jedidiah Tingle.

Harmon, a real estate developer, had become a millionaire by offering property for a dollar down and a payment of a few cents a week, on tracts of land that he owned and had improved. It provided an opportunity for lower-income folks to own a home and tapped a market that until then was unknown. By 1900 he had offices in both Massachusetts and New York and that year invested four million dollars in new building sites in Brooklyn.

He was quoted as saying, "The gift of land is the gift eternal," and he created the Harmon Foundation to buy land in communities so children would have playgrounds. He also set up a foundation to recognize African American achievements in the arts, science, business, and agriculture.

His hometown of Lebanon was not forgotten. His very first playground was built there in 1911. Harmon Hall, the home of the Warren County Historical Society, was another gift to the community. William Elmer Harmon died in 1928, but the Harmon Civic Trust he endowed specifically for ongoing community improvement projects in Lebanon still exists today.

So why did he sign his grandfather's name, Jedidiah Tingle, to many of his donations? Some say it was just his sense of humor and perhaps a desire for anonymity; others claim it was his Midwest values and a unique way to honor Jedidiah, who had been an early Ohio settler. Whatever the reason, William Elmer Harmon found a way to give a gift that keeps on giving.

The Grapes of Ohio

CINCINNATI

Who would imagine that a man who believed in temperance, who was disgusted with people who drank too much liquor, would create the American wine industry and even have one of his wines praised in a poem by one of America's most famous poets?

It happened in Ohio.

People have been making wine forever, of course. It probably started when some caveman found some fermented wild grapes, scarfed them down, and enjoyed a slight buzz from the concoction.

Wine is prominently mentioned in the Bible and was a drink of choice of many cultures through the ages.

By the eighteenth century grapes had been domesticated in Europe and were producing the finest wines then known in the world.

But American grapes were different. They were a different species, and they were mostly wild. They didn't make good wine or raisins; they weren't very good served fresh. Early colonists called them "fox grapes" because they smelled like a fox, especially after they had fermented, and if you have ever smelled a fox, you know it was not a pleasant smell. They were pretty much ignored except by a few stubborn folks who still tried to make wine from them.

Efforts had been made many times to import European grapevines, but the climate, disease, and blight killed them every time.

That was when Nicholas Longworth of Cincinnati came on the scene. He was called "Old Nick" by his friends. A self-made man who had become an attorney and often accepted property as a payment for his services, he eventually found himself one of the biggest landowners in the country, and one of the richest. He was looking for a hobby, and he liked to grow things. He bought some grapevine clippings from a friend of Thomas Jefferson. The vines produced the grape we today call Catawba.

At first the wine wasn't very good, but Old Nick had the money and time to keep trying. He experimented. He tried separating the skins from the juice before fermenting. What resulted was a Catawba wine that his mainly German-speaking neighbors loved. It reminded them of the table wines at home. He had a hit on his hands.

Now bear in mind Nicholas Longworth didn't approve of drinking. At that time in America, with drinking water unsafe in cities and milk that could easily spoil or carry diseases, there was little left to drink but whiskey, which usually was readily available and, presumably, safe to drink but could have undesirable results. By creating a good dry table wine that was about 12 percent alcohol, he believed he was doing his bit for temperance, as well as making some money with his hobby.

He was so involved now with winemaking that he gave up his legal practice to spend all his time developing his vineyards. He was on a crusade to change America's drinking habits. With his wealth he was able to buy more and more land to plant grapevines. He didn't know how to make sparkling wines, so he brought in French winemakers from Champagne to show him how it was done. The result was a sparkling Catawba wine that rivaled French Champagne in the eyes of some American Easterners who would never before drink American wines.

Nicholas Longworth had started the American wine industry. By the mid-1850s his wineries were producing more than 100,000 bottles a year. Easterners were consuming them and spreading the word about Ohio wines.

But as Old Nick's wine business started to blossom, so did the temperance movement. And much to Longworth's consternation, the movement had decided to oppose consumption of alcohol in all forms. Prohibition was the new cry across the country. In 1853 Samuel Carey, also former Cincinnati attorney and farmer, campaigned to stop the sale of all alcoholic beverages in Ohio. Longworth suddenly found himself on the other side of the fence. He fought Carey publicly on the question of Prohibition and spent a great deal of money to defeat the issue. Longworth was the victor at the ballot box, but from then on Carey and Longworth were enemies.

Wine was now big business for Old Nick. In 1859 Ohio produced more than 570,000 gallons, twice as much as California. In fact, at that time Ohio supplied one-third of the nation's entire wine output.

Then another crisis occurred. In 1860 black rot and downy mildew struck the vineyards of Ohio. The Catawba grapes were especially susceptible, and there was no cure. The vines began to die. While Longworth's wealth kept him afloat, the American wine industry, which had been centered in Cincinnati and southern Ohio and had once attracted people from all over the world, was in a tailspin. Then in 1863, Nicholas Longworth, the man who had started it all and was the driving force behind the industry, died.

Without Old Nick and his passionate drive, the next decade saw the wine industry in southern Ohio drying up to just a trickle. A new winegrowing area near the Lake Erie Islands had been discovered, and winemaking in Ohio moved north.

Nicholas Longworth was much loved in Cincinnati. He gave to charity but said he didn't want to help "the Lord's poor" because he felt that needy people like starving widows with children would get plenty of help. He wanted to assist the ones he called "the devil's poor." It was perhaps with his temperance beliefs in mind that he said, "I will help the devil's poor, the miserable drunken dog that nobody else will do anything for but despise and kick."

He donated four acres of choice land in downtown Cincinnati to the Cincinnati Astronomical Society so they could build an observatory. Artists in the Cincinnati area also received financial help from Old Nick.

Nicholas Longworth, the man who started America's wine industry, is only sparsely remembered in history books, and he is often confused with one of his descendants, also named Nicholas Longworth, who married Teddy Roosevelt's daughter.

But it was the original Nicholas Longworth, Old Nick, who created a wine so good that American literary giant Henry Wadsworth Longfellow was moved to write a lyrical ode about his favorite drink:

> *For richest and best*
> *Is the wine of the West.*
> *That grows by the Beautiful River;*
> *Whose sweet perfume*
> *Fills all the room*
> *With a benison on the giver . . .*
> *While pure as a spring*
> *Is the wine I sing,*
> *And to praise it, one needs but name it;*
> *For Catawba wine*
> *Has need of no sign,*
> *No tavern-bush to proclaim it.*
> *And this Song of the Vine,*
> *This greeting of mine,*
> *The winds and the birds shall deliver*
> *To the Queen of the West,*
> *In her garlands dressed,*
> *On the banks of the Beautiful River.*
> —"Ode to Catawba Wine"

Mr. Wilks's Hill

HAMILTON

All Harry Wilks of Hamilton originally wanted to do was to build his dream home. He acquired forty acres of rolling wooded land that overlooked the Great Miami River in Butler County.

His dream home turned out to be an extraordinary seven-thousand-square-foot underground home built into the side of a hill. It was a showcase just right to display his collection of antique sculptures from places like Greece, Egypt, and Italy.

He began to develop the property, building roads, landscaping, and installing lakes and ponds. The development started to attract local businessmen, who asked him to sell lots off his land so they could also build homes there.

Wilks wasn't interested. In fact, he realized that if he didn't do anything about it, the woodland environment he prized so much might become just another suburban housing development. So he decided to acquire even more surrounding land and create a public park. But not just any kind of park: a sculpture park exhibiting a wonderful balance between art and nature on 265 acres.

In 1995 Wilks donated all the land and much of his personal collection of sculptures to a new nonprofit organization that became known as Pyramid Hill Sculpture Park and Museum, giving the Hamilton area of southwest Ohio a cultural treasure and also a tourist attraction. It's one of only three major outdoor sculpture parks in the United States.

Now, appreciation of modern art is in the eye of the beholder, and I will be the first to admit that sometimes when I look upon some of these huge pieces of public art all I can think is, What was the artist thinking?

On Harry Wilks's hillside are gathered nearly forty enormous outdoor artworks. The largest is a piece by Alexander Liberman, a giant red-colored steel sculpture called *Abracadabra*. It's said to be so large that airplanes flying far overhead can see it. The piece, three-and-a-half stories wide and two-and-a-half stories high, sits atop a hill in the middle of the park. There is also the Jon Isherwood piece *The Age of Stone*, which combines ancient forms with contemporary materials.

Then there is the sculpture that looks like two giant metal springs, called *Looking at It—Looking from It* by Clasina Van Bemmel.

Despite the striking appearance of many of these artworks, they do seem to blend together in this terrain, which has become one of three major outdoor art parks in the United States.

While all Harry Wilks wanted to do was to build a home where he could enjoy his art treasures, what he did instead was to give a priceless gift to the Buckeye State.

The Pyramid Hill Sculpture Park and Museum is located on State Route 128, Hamilton-Cleves Road, one mile south of Hamilton, Ohio. It is open to the public Tuesday through Sunday. www.pyramidhill.org

America's Oldest Veteran
BELLE VALLEY

In his dreams before he died, he could still hear the boom of cannons, the volleys of musket fire, the screams of the injured. Like many American men in 1868, he had seen war. But this veteran was unique.

His name was John Gray, and he was not a veteran of the recently ended Civil War—he was the last living veteran of the American Revolutionary War.

Gray lived most of his life in Noble County, Ohio, and he died there as well. He would have died in abject poverty had it not been for the efforts of another veteran—a veteran of the Civil War.

Incredibly, Gray was born on George Washington's plantation, Mount Vernon, in Virginia. His family worked as day laborers for Washington. When the war came and Washington took command of the Continental forces, Gray's father joined him. Gray's father was killed at the battle of White Plains, and John, although only age 17 at the time, immediately enlisted. He came under fire by the British at Williamsburg, and he was at Yorktown when Cornwallis surrendered.

After the war ended he went back to Mount Vernon, but since he was not a landowner, under Virginia law he could not vote. On the advice of George Washington, Gray set out for the wilds of Kentucky and Ohio, where he could clear and claim some land. He eventually settled near Brookfield, in Noble County, and built a cabin and operated a small farm.

John Gray lived a long life, dying at 104 years of age. He and a stepdaughter still lived in the small cabin, but advancing age and ill health had brought them to the edge of poverty.

A Civil War veteran, J. L. Dalzell, who as a child used to play on Gray's farm, rallied veterans of his own war when he discovered Gray

Perhaps John Gray, who fought with George Washington, looked grouchy in this picture because Congress didn't get around to giving him a pension until he was 103 years old.

received no pension for his services to the Continental Army. But the bureaucracy in Washington was just as bad then as now. It took weeks and months for bureaucrats to trace Gray's history, to confirm that he actually had served in the Revolutionary War, that he was who he claimed to be and not just an old soldier living out a fantasy. But it was all true: he had known Washington; he had been on the bloody field at Williamsburg. Just one year before he died Gray finally was granted a pension from the U.S. Congress. How much was it? A little less than $50 a month.

John Gray, the man who fought for our independence and who also watched Ohio become a state, is buried in a small cemetery about 250 yards from where his cabin stood on Brookfield Township Road. There are two markers. One is a fading stone that calls Gray "One of Washington's compatriots." The other, a modern military grave marker, simply says:

John Gray
Continental Line
Rev. War
Born Jan 6, 1764
Died Mar 29 1868

The graveyard is difficult to locate; there is a modern-day monument dedicated to Gray located in a former roadside park on State Route 821 south of the town of Belle Valley. For more information contact the Noble County Tourism Board at 740-732-2191, www.noblecountyohio.com

SOUTHEAST OHIO

The Waterloo Wonders

WATERLOO

We Buckeyes love our basketball. Remember the excitement over LeBron James during his high school days? The amazing Akron youngster was the biggest thing to hit high school basketball in years, leading his team to three state championships, and the excitement continued when he decided to forgo college and begin a professional career with the Cleveland Cavaliers.

By the time James was 18 years old he was being deluged with offers to be the spokesman for various products and offered wads of money. He could afford designer clothes and drive a $60,000 sport-utility vehicle. But the nice thing about LeBron James is that he loves the game of basketball, and it shows. The fact that he is paid well to play the game is just icing on the cake.

There have been other Ohio kids who displayed great talent on the basketball court, but their only reward was the proverbial fifteen minutes of fame—no endorsements, no commercials. Time has erased the cheering crowds and the bright lights, and the dust of years has dimmed the trophies, the brilliance of their accomplishments now fading like the sound of a bouncing basketball in an empty gymnasium.

If you saw the movie *Hoosiers* you know the plot: The little rural school where basketball was the obsession. A once-in-a-lifetime season when they went on to win the big game and the championship against all kinds of obstacles.

That story was fiction, based on some real-life events in Indiana. But the screenwriters missed an even better story, a story that actually happened in Ohio: the story of the Waterloo Wonders.

Waterloo, Ohio, hasn't changed much since it was the talk of Ohio and much of the sporting world in the mid-1930s.

The little community in Lawrence County straddles the Gallia County line. Ironton, the county seat, is the closest "big town" to Waterloo. It's the kind of place where the kids could go to see a movie or take a date for dinner on a weekend.

The first signs of what was to come happened in 1932, at the height of the Great Depression.

A young man with the wonderful name of Magellan Hairston signed on at the tiny Waterloo High School as principal. Teachers and administrators at the high school wore several hats, as they often did at small rural schools in those days. Magellan Hairston was also the coach of the high school basketball team. That year, to everyone's surprise, the team won enough games to become the Lawrence County champions.

Understand that in the 1920s and '30s Ohio's rural school systems were just evolving from one-room schoolhouses and two-year "academies" to what were then called "centralized schools." In other words, the communities were combining several one-room schools into a central school building that usually held grades 1 through 12 and had enough rooms to separate the classes. Many of the schools had a combination gymnasium and auditorium, usually a cracker-box-sized gym with a tiny stage at one side. The room was used for basketball but could be easily converted into a meeting room or theater, often for community events.

These schools produced the teams that played in what was then called the Class B state basketball league. Waterloo High School's total male enrollment of twenty-six gave the coach a very limited pool of talent to draw on for a basketball team. Most of these kids were from farm families. Before the local gymnasium was built, their basketball courts were outdoors, the court just a flat patch of dirt, probably clay, that had been graded and pounded smooth; the basket was often an old tire ring fastened to makeshift backboards on the side of the school building.

So winning the county championship for the very first time was a big event for Waterloo. It was mostly ignored by the media outside of Lawrence County, though. That was soon to change.

Despite their glum looks, these young men had become a legend in Ohio high school basketball. They were the "Waterloo Wonders."

Magellan Hairston's starting team for the 1933 school year was made up of kids who had spent their preteen years playing together on the outdoor dirt-floor courts. Their basketball in some cases was just a bunch of old rags bound together with tape. These were kids who loved the game so much that, after putting in a full day doing farm chores, they would walk ten miles to another community for the chance to shoot baskets in a community gymnasium.

There was Beryl Drummond, who at five feet, seven inches tall had been considered too small to play basketball at nearby Cadmus High School and had transferred to Waterloo, hoping for a chance to be able to play.

Curtis McMahon had played under coach Hairston in 1931 when Hairston was the coach in nearby Windsor. When his father died in 1932, McMahon moved to Waterloo to live with an uncle. He was looking forward to the chance to play for Hairston again.

Then there were the two cousins: Orlyn Roberts, who was nearly six feet tall and had been center of the 1932 county championship team, and his cousin Wyman Roberts. Both boys spent long hours in the summer practicing in a makeshift basketball court in the hay-mow of a relative's barn.

The fifth member of the squad, Stewart Wiseman, was the son of the former Waterloo coach Frank Wiseman, who had retired, creating the opening for Magellan Hairston. Stewart Wiseman lived on a farm five miles from Waterloo and created his own basketball court in a pasture near his home, using a horse-drawn iron scraper to smooth the ground. He was able to rig a basket at one end for his practice shots every summer's day that the weather permitted it.

Magellan Hairston and his five starters captured the Lawrence County championship for the second year in a row. In their twenty-game season, they never lost once. And it didn't stop there. They also took on Rio Grande College and a freshman team from Marshall College in West Virginia, handing both defeats. Now, sportswriters were starting to take note.

The *Ironton Tribune* wrote: "Coach Magellan Hairston has something at Waterloo High School this year. If he isn't grooming a state championship squad in that back country section, then a majority of Lawrence County residents will be disappointed."

Then came the sectional tournament, and the Waterloo five romped over every opponent and in five games had become the sectional champion and earned a berth at the district tournament, one step away from the state championship games in Columbus.

Folks were really starting to believe that this little country school where the kids had learned to play basketball on an often muddy outdoor court using a tape-wrapped bundle of rags for a ball might actually have a shot at the state championship.

Eight teams gathered at Ohio University at Athens for the district playoffs. It all came down to a final game between New Boston High School and Waterloo. Something was wrong that night. No one is sure quite what, but the Waterloo five were off their usual pace. By the third period they were tied with New Boston. It looked like the drive for the state title might come to an end. But then, in the last part of the third period, Waterloo seemed to come alive. Wyman Roberts, McMahon, and Wiseman finally gave them an eight-point lead to take into the final quarter.

Starting the last eight minutes, Drummond and Orlyn Roberts each scored two points, followed by a New Boston bucket. They now had a ten-point lead. But New Boston kept challenging and, with only seconds to go in a hard-fought game, had whittled the lead down to only five points. The boys from Waterloo managed to hang on, and when the horn sounded, even though they had just played perhaps the worst game of their season, they were the district champions and for the first time in their young lives were headed for Columbus and a chance to become number one in the state.

Many sportswriters had taken to calling them the Waterloo Wonders, and it was about this time that some of the myths began to spread about the team.

Perhaps the wildest rumor was that the entire team was made up of grown men in their twenties just pretending to be high school boys. Some sportswriters figured that was the only possible explanation for the perfect season that the Waterloo team had so far recorded.

That was nonsense, of course; all the boys were still in high school and under the required age limit for playing high school basketball.

There was a report that they had all been imported from other areas of the state and didn't have to attend classes; all they had to do was play basketball and win games.

That, too, was silly, since the Roberts cousins had lived all their lives in Waterloo, and Wiseman was the son of the former coach. They attended class like any other teenagers. Some were better students than others, but all had passing grades.

As for reports of smoking and drinking and other high jinks, their coach, years later, told writers that as far as he knew the boys did not break his training rules and that they were some of the best-conditioned athletes he had ever worked with.

That training, some of it self-imposed, was about to pay off. Anyone who has ever played basketball on a rough surface knows how hard it is to handle and dribble the ball. When these country boys got onto a glass-smooth hardwood floor, they were experts. They didn't do much dribbling, and instead of passing the ball like other players, they fired it to each other like a baseball, the extra energy in each pass probably resulting from those years of trying to throw a ball made of rags and tape. And they were a team in every sense of the word. They knew each other's moves. They could pass the ball without even looking, knowing their teammate would be where the ball was thrown. Magellan Hairston had also made sure that no one player was the star. Each was capable of making baskets and of swift ball handling. All were stars, these Waterloo Wonders.

The five starters packed themselves into Coach Hairston's old

Chevrolet for the hundred-mile ride to the state capital. The rest of the team and their supporters followed in a school bus. This was the first time the boys had been in a city as large and as busy as Columbus, and it was an experience they would never forget. Like many small-town tourists, they gawked at the buildings and the busy streets and probably felt like outsiders. But that evening, as they put on their black-and-white uniforms and trotted onto the biggest basketball court they had ever played on, they settled down and played like a well-oiled machine.

Coach Hairston, though, didn't sound so positive. In an interview before the game he told a sportswriter, "If you want to see us play, you better come to the first game."

But the Waterloo Wonders were there to win. They defeated their first opponent, Chandlersville, from Muskingham County, 58-29. Their next opponent was Lowellville, whom they downed 43-32, leaving only the team from Mark Center, Ohio, standing between them and the Ohio Class B title.

March 21, 1934. For the third time that week the black-and-white-uniformed Waterloo Wonders ran onto the Coliseum floor at the fairgrounds. Over seven thousand people filled the stands. Cheerleaders were leading the crowd in a chant:

A basket, a basket, a basket, boys.
You make the basket.
We'll make the noise!

Orlyn Roberts was on a roll that night. In the first half he had sunk basket after basket, accounting for many of the twenty points that Waterloo scored, as compared to eleven for Mark Center.

But in the third quarter Mark Center closed the gap to a single basket, and the Waterloo fans who had been rocking the Coliseum with their cheers suddenly became very quiet.

Were they going to get this far, this close to a first-ever state championship, only to lose it in the last minutes of the game?

But suddenly Waterloo exploded: Orlyn Roberts sank a pair, followed by cousin Wyman, and then Orlyn again, followed this time by McMahon, who closed the third quarter with Waterloo ahead 30–19.

The fourth quarter was anticlimactic. Orlyn Roberts would go on to set a tournament record with a three-game total of sixty-nine points. Mark Center would lose by a score of 40–26.

When the final horn blew, fans came spilling out of the stands and onto the floor. The impossible had happened. Little Waterloo, Ohio, from the backwoods of southern Ohio was the new state champion.

But the team's story wasn't over yet.

The start of the 1934-35 season found all the starting players on the Waterloo Wonders still together, three of them in their senior year. They were still basking in the glow of their victory, perhaps becoming a bit cocky. They were playing Class A teams now, and even some college teams, as well as their regular B league opponents—and easily defeating all of them.

The Waterloo boys had learned how to entertain the crowd, especially when the contest was one-sided. They would sometimes win the tip-off at center court and then offer the ball to the opposing side and invite them to have a free shot at the basket. Or when they were well ahead they sometimes would turn and make a basket for the other team, much to the crowd's delight and the frustration of the team they were playing.

On other occasions, two or three of the players would leave the floor to sit on the sidelines and play cards or eat popcorn, while the remaining team members took on five opponents.

They would make passes behind the back, or through an opponent's legs. They would sometimes roll the ball across the floor until it rolled up the leg of a teammate, who would then quickly make a basket while the other side stood stunned by the fancy ball-handling.

They truly were wonders.

But then it happened. Their long winning streak came to an end.

Some people say it was poor officiating, others say the boys had gotten overconfident and careless. In any event, they found themselves in a close game with Greenfield-McClain High School from Highland County. It was a well-fought contest that ended in a tie and went into sudden-death overtime. The overflow crowd, mostly Greenfield-McClain supporters who had come to see their team play the Wonders, had spilled over onto the edge of the playing floor. Wyman Roberts made a two-handed shot from the side of the floor while being jostled by fans. The ball whipped through the net, for what they believed was the winning basket, only to have officials nullify the points because he had touched a spectator as he shot. Moments later Greenfield-McClain got lucky, and the game was over; the Waterloo Wonders had their first defeat.

But it didn't seem to faze the boys from Waterloo. They took the defeat in their stride and continued on their campaign to repeat their statewide victory the year before.

Everyone wanted to play them now. Wherever they went, they drew crowds. One of their more amazing feats was the night that through a scheduling error they were slated to play teams in both Jackson and Chesapeake. They decided to keep the schedule and play two games against two opponents, the same evening.

At 7 P.M., they hosted Chesapeake at Waterloo. The Wonders came onto the floor and devastated the Chesapeake team. When they had built up what they considered a good lead, the starters left the floor, leaving their junior varsity members to handle the foundering Chesapeake team. The Wonders jumped in Coach Hairston's car and sped off to Jackson, where a crowd was waiting to watch them play their second game of the night. The final score against Chesapeake was 45–5; on the same night Waterloo also beat Jackson 45–24.

This was a once-in-a-lifetime team, and no one doubted they would be in the state finals for the second year in a row.

And that is exactly what happened. On March 23, 1935, they returned to the Coliseum in Columbus to meet the Oxford Stewart Tigers, who also had had a nearly unblemished season. It was going to be a close match, according to sportswriters of the time. By the end of the first quarter it looked like the predictions were coming true. The score was tied 8–8.

In the second quarter the Wonders changed their strategy and shifted to a man-to-man defense. Wyman Roberts and Beryl Drummond both dumped in shots to end the half with Waterloo in the lead 17–13.

By the fourth quarter, the game had seesawed back and forth, and Waterloo was ahead by only four points. But it was enough. In the final seconds McMahon got a point with a single free throw, and the Tigers came back with two more, but the final score was Waterloo 25, Oxford Stewart 22.

The Waterloo Wonders were state champions for the second year in a row.

* * *

The Waterloo Wonders were, at that time, only the second team in state history to win a state championship two years in a row (Bellepoint High School had done it in the 1920s). With the media attention they were now getting, they had plenty of offers to travel and give exhibition games. They tried to oblige everyone they could.

There was the game in Painesville, Ohio, one snowy night. They started out on the long drive across the state on pre-interstate roads. The storm got worse. When they reached Columbus they called the Painesville school and said they might not be able to keep their date at the school. The school official told them that the building was sold out and the crowd would wait for them. They pressed on through the storm, but it was slow going, and they did not reach Painesville until 1:00 in the morning. As they approached on the snow-covered roads, through the snowflakes they could see the lights were still on in the school, and the crowd inside was still waiting for them. They got a standing ovation as they walked in. They also won the game.

In the sports world of today, players such as these would probably be scouted by colleges from all over the country. They would be offered scholarships and most likely a chance to play for professional basketball teams and get contracts worth millions. A coach and mentor like Magellan Hairston would probably be offered jobs coaching college or university teams and even be considered for professional coaching jobs. I'd like to tell you that is what happened. But it did not.

Graduation that spring broke up the Wonders. Three of the boys, Orlyn Roberts, Curtis McMahon, and Stewart Wiseman, all received their diplomas. Wyman Roberts and Beryl Drummond would have another year to play, but the new team never again matched their seasons of 1934 and 1935.

Magellan Hairston became embroiled in a dispute with school board officials about accounting for the money the team had received from exhibition games and from schools they had visited. The dispute was fueled by some sloppy bookkeeping, jealousy, and even politics. The coach was eventually absolved of any wrongdoing, but Hairston, angered over the challenge to his integrity, resigned. He would return under a new administration in 1938, and in 1941 he would coach a Waterloo team that again made it to the state finals, though this time they were defeated. After the war he left teaching and became an automobile dealer.

Some of the Wonders played in a semiprofessional basketball league. In 1937 at Cleveland's Public Hall they took on the New York Celtics, then the best in the professional world, and beat them 47 to 39.

World War II interrupted many of their lives, and after the war the boys, one by one, gave up basketball. Stewart Wiseman went to college and became a teacher. The others turned to factory and farm work to make a living.

In 1996 coach Magellan Hairston was inducted posthumously into the Ohio High School Basketball Coaches Hall of Fame

All of them are gone now. Coach Magellan Hairston died in 1968. He was 61.

Beryl Drummond and Orlyn Roberts both passed away in 1983. Wyman Roberts was 72 when he died in 1985. Curtis McMahon died in April of 1978. The last of the Wonders to leave us was Stewart Wiseman, who was 79 when he died in 1996.

In 1960 Waterloo High School ceased to exist when it was consolidated into the Symmes Valley School System.

A few years ago, the old Waterloo High School building was abandoned.

A basket, a basket, a basket, boys.
You make the basket.
We'll make the noise.

The only noise these days is the occasional roar of a car driving by on Ohio Route 141, near where it all started, where some Ohio farm kids used to play on a dirt court with a ball made of rags wrapped in tape. All that is left is a bronze historical marker that commemorates them and their achievements.

They truly were the Waterloo Wonders.

The Mysterious Ring

AVA

It was a hot summer's morning in June 1937. A Mrs. Larrison was in her garden at her rented farm home, just east of the tiny town of Ava, Ohio.

As she pulled at some weeds she noticed something shiny. There on the stem of a wild mustard plant was a man's gold ring.

It was a massive ring with an onyx stone. Inside, the ring was inscribed with the name of the owner, Zachary Lansdowne.

The discovery, it turns out, was the final chapter in a tragedy that had occurred in the Ohio skies over the Larrison home twelve years earlier.

Early on the morning of September 3, 1925, Commander Zachary Lansdowne, a native of Greenville, Ohio, and captain of the U.S. Navy airship *Shenandoah*, was asleep in his quarters when a giant Ohio thunderstorm slammed into his ship while it was flying over Cambridge, Ohio.

The huge *Shenandoah* was America's first rigid airship filled with nonflammable helium. It was 682 feet long and weighed 41 tons. To put it in perspective, the *Shenandoah* was as long as two football fields placed end to end. Its top speed was sixty miles per hour.

The *Shenandoah* was on a three-thousand-mile "goodwill" flight over several midwestern states to show off the navy's newest airship to the American people. Lansdowne, who had grown up in Ohio,

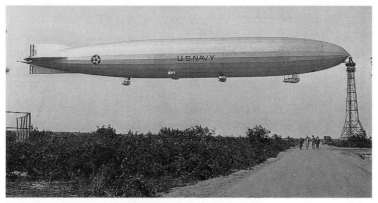

"Daughter of the stars," the U.S. Navy airship Shenandoah.

It was at the scene of the Shenandoah's crash, near Ava, Ohio, that Commander Lansdowne's ring mysteriously disappeared only to turn up in a nearby garden years later.

was familiar with the increased possibility of late-summer thunderstorms and violent weather in the area and had urged his superiors to delay the flight, but he was overruled by navy brass who wanted to take advantage of crowds at late-summer fairs and festivals.

So on this early September morning, with no modern radar to warn them of the severity of the approaching storm and only primitive radio facilities, already blurred by constant static from the lightning, the *Shenandoah* and her crew stumbled into a life-and-death battle with the forces of nature over a remote Ohio countryside.

It was about 3 A.M. when crewmembers became concerned about the wind and frequent lightning of the gathering storm and aroused Lansdowne, who had been sleeping. He immediately dressed and came down to the control car suspended beneath the giant cigar-shaped ship.

At just before 5 A.M. Commander Lansdowne started to lose control of the ship, which was being buffeted by heavy winds and rain. The ship, caught in powerful updrafts, started to rise uncontrollably. It had risen almost six thousand feet when finally the release of some helium stopped the ascension, but then just as quickly a downdraft caught the ship, and it plunged in a freefall toward the earth. Lansdowne ordered the release of more than four thousand pounds of water ballast to slow the descent. It helped, and by the time they had sunk to three thousand feet the ship seemed to be leveling off

and was back under control. But seconds later a new, larger air mass grabbed the ship and pushed it up, this time at an incredible speed. The silver airship, almost standing on its tail, started to spin toward the heavens as cables and girders in the interior started to saw back and forth, making a screaming noise that nearly drowned out the wind and motors.

Then it happened. The *Shenandoah* began to come apart. Commander Lansdowne, sensing they were doomed, told his men that they could leave the control car for the possible relative safety of the interior of the ship if they wanted to. Two men scrambled out; the rest stayed with Lansdowne.

There were several violent shudders that shook the ship, and then the control car broke loose and plummeted toward earth. Commander Lansdowne and the eleven men who chose to stay with him were all killed on impact.

The stern, or tail section, of the airship came gently down to tree-top level and drifted west toward the town of Ava, finally catching in a tree with a jolt that dumped out four crewmen, who, although dazed by the fall, survived. The tail section broke loose again and drifted to a nearby small valley, where it settled on the ground, and eighteen members of the crew were able to literally step out of the wreckage unhurt.

The front section of the *Shenandoah* continued to fly for another twelve miles southwest of the breakup site. Seven crewmembers were inside, hanging onto ropes. It finally floated to earth on the Ernest Nichols farm. Nichols heard the cries of the crewmen and grabbed a dangling rope, tying it around a fence post. But a gust of wind moved the derelict ship, and it tore the fence post out of the ground. Nichols then wrapped the rope around a tree stump, forcing the huge broken air ship to flutter down on a nearby hillside, and six more men walked out of the wreckage. (Another man also survived; he had been knocked off his rope when the floating wreck hit the tree over Nichols's farm.).

The final toll was fourteen dead and twenty-nine survivors.

Rescue workers and the curious started pouring into the area. The dead were covered with blankets and left for a while where they fell; later they were taken to the front porch of the nearby home of Andy Gamary, a Noble County farmer. They eventually were moved to the neighboring community of Belle Valley, where they were deposited at a funeral home.

There, while the process of identifying the victims was going on, it was noticed that Commander Lansdowne's Naval Academy ring was missing. A search was made of the area where he fell to earth, but the ring was not found. Most believed that it had either been lost in the debris of the crash or, perhaps, taken by a looter. In the first hours after the crash there was very little security at the site, and onlookers were able to walk freely through the twisted metal taking what they wanted.

A Naval Academy class ring is an important part of a midshipman's life and is usually treasured by both the owner and his family. Each class at the academy designs its own ring, and the jeweler who manufactures the ring has to sign an agreement to never make a similar ring for anyone who is not a member of that class. Most naval officers wear their rings with pride throughout their careers

So when Mrs. Larrison discovered Commander Lansdowne's ring in her garden twelve years after the crash, it was an important find.

Just how important, Mrs. Larrison soon found out. She called the Noble County sheriff's office. They in turn called the Federal Bureau of Investigation in Washington, D.C., and it wasn't long before two FBI agents arrived to take the ring back to Washington. The head of the FBI, J. Edgar Hoover, personally delivered the ring to Commander Lansdowne's widow.

But according to Bryan Rayner of Ava, Ohio, the discovery of Commander Lansdowne's ring was not the end of the story.

Rayner, who operates a garage and towing service in Ava, is probably one of the most knowledgeable people in Ohio when it comes to the *Shenandoah*. Both of his grandfathers were at the crash site. His family owns much of the land where pieces of the airship landed, and he and his wife, Theresa, operate a small museum in a camping trailer filled with *Shenandoah* memorabilia that they tow around to area schools to keep the memory of the airship alive.

According to Rayner, Commander Lansdowne's grandson and other relatives have visited Ava and told him that before Lansdowne left on his last voyage aboard the *Shenandoah* the onyx stone in his ring was cracked and loose. Yet when the ring was returned to the family twelve years later, after being found in Mrs. Larrison's garden, the stone was in perfect condition and undamaged. "A lot of folks just couldn't believe that a ring could lay out in the weeds and weather for twelve years," said Bryan Rayner, "and be in as good a condition as that ring was when it was found."

Did the commander have the ring repaired just before the last journey? No one knows for sure, but there are also those that suspect the ring may have been stolen from his body and repaired, and then years later, for some reason—perhaps guilt—brought back to the area where it was taken and placed in the Larrison garden.

The Shadow

BARNESVILLE

They held a memorial service in Barnesville, Ohio, for an old friend; about forty people from all over the United States attended. The service was held outdoors, near a corral. That was very appropriate, because the deceased had spent many happy hours on this southern Ohio cattle ranch.

The memorial program quoted the psalms, especially Psalm 112:9 ("his horn shall be exalted with honor"). The selection was very fitting, for the dearly departed was, in fact, a bull.

Now mind you, this wasn't just any bull. "The Shadow" was a tremendous longhorn steer weighing more than a ton, with horns spreading more than five feet from tip to tip. Pictures of him in his

The Shadow was perhaps the only bull in the country that commuted to work in Texas and Ohio.

prime attest to the fact that he was an imposing figure, his dark-brown coloring looking almost black. Against a skyline he did, indeed, resemble a giant shadow.

The Shadow was born on June 6, 1991, in Calhan, Colorado, on one of the Dickinson Cattle Company ranches. When he was six months old, he was purchased by a man in Fresno, California.

His original name was "the Veep"—for vice president. (His father's name had been Senator, and somehow a bull named after a politician seems very appropriate.)

But as the Veep began to grow, the huge body and the massive horn spread began to stir talk in the longhorn industry. The Dickinson Cattle Company, which had moved its headquarters to a ranch in Belmont County, Ohio, decided that perhaps they had made a mistake in selling the bull. So owner Kirk Dickinson drove out to Fresno to take another look at the now-grown bull. What he saw he liked, and a deal was struck. Veep was loaded into Dickinson's truck and came back to the Colorado ranch for a while and then to Ohio to his new home.

It was here that ranch hands started calling him the Shadow because of his massive profile and horn spread, which now reached an incredible eighty-two inches.

But it wasn't only his impressive horns. In the spring of 1998 the first calves fathered by the Shadow were born, and as they began to grow, they began to show their heritage with horn spreads of more than sixty inches before their third birthday, many of them also black brindles with dark colors, much like their old man. The Shadow's fame was such by now that, with the modern marvel of artificial insemination, he was fathering calves all over America. (His frozen semen was now valued three times higher than a comparable amount of gold.) This was not an ordinary bull.

But the Shadow paid a heavy price for his productivity. He was plagued by injuries in the pursuit of his pleasure. In 1999 he punctured a toe, and the toe had to be removed. Then arthritis set in, and veterinarians had to prescribe special medications to relieve his pain. By the summer of 2002 the big bull was crippled in three legs. He passed away on April 24, 2003.

But the Shadow will live on in the young calves that he will father for years to come. Because of his productivity his frozen semen is still being used to breed new steers across the country.

A memorial stone marker can be seen just outside the corral at the Dickinson Cattle Company Ranch on Muskrat Road in Barnesville, Ohio. During the summer months, public tours of the ranch are offered.

A Man of the River

MARIETTA

At the end of the 1970s I had just started hosting a new travel program called *One Tank Trips* at WJW television in Cleveland.

I had chosen Marietta, Ohio, for one of the inaugural trips. I had never been to Marietta but had heard that it was a charming river town steeped in history.

Not knowing anyone, I decided to just take a camera crew and go there, searching out attractions after we arrived. My welcome to the community was less than auspicious.

My first stop was the local convention and visitor bureau. An elderly lady behind the counter stared at me with a less-than-friendly look when I announced that I was in the town looking to do a story about "one tank trips."

"We don't have any dealings with the army here," she said.

Confused, I tried to explain that I wasn't with the army, but she was still fixated on the word *tank*.

"What do you want with an army tank?" she asked.

I again tried to explain, but she suggested we head for Fort Knox in Kentucky if we wanted to see tanks. I gave up, and we left.

My crew and I drove around the town, hoping something would catch our eye.

We were on the edge of the Muskingum River when suddenly I heard the sound of a ship's bell and heard rhythmic splashing. We looked to the left, and there was a vision out of the past. The twin smokestacks towering black against the sky, the stage protruding like a tongue from the front of the boat. And at the rear, a giant wheel churning the water and splashing rainbows into the springtime sun. The white ship with red trim had people lining every deck. The name on the pilothouse was *The Valley Gem*. The pilot, wearing a cowboy hat, returned our wave, and when he docked a few minutes later he motioned us to come aboard as his passengers left the ship.

That was my first meeting with Captain James Sands, Sr., owner, pilot and captain of the sternwheeler *Valley Gem*.

River men are legends. The men who sail the great rivers of America have written many pages of our history and become larger than life.

Mike Fink was perhaps the first man to work on the Ohio River who entered this category. He was born on the river in the 1770s, probably near Pittsburgh, and worked as a keelboat man on the flatboats that were the early freighters of the rivers. There have been so many exaggerations about his life that it's often hard to tell what is the truth. We do know that he was killed in a shooting somewhere near the mouth of the Yellowstone River. In his life he was a skilled river pilot, an expert shooter, a fighter, and a champion teller of tall tales. He became sort of the great-great-grandfather of that entire rough, tough breed that calls themselves "river men."

Some say you have to be born on the river. But Captain James E. Sands, Sr., proved that's not so. Sands was a big, burly, gruff man who said what he thought and meant what he said. And he carved out a niche for himself on the river, especially the river that flows past Ohio's earliest city.

Jim Sands, the man who brought back the thrill of riding a paddlewheel boat to Ohio's first city, Marietta.

Sands was born in Columbus. He ended up living in Marietta in 1948 because his father's contracting business, Shelly and Sands, had just built a plant in the river city. Jim was only there a short time. He moved away from Marietta to attend Miami University.

While playing football for Miami, he broke his neck. His football days were over, and he transferred to Marietta College.

There, a doctor suggested that rowing crew, on one of those speedy, sleek rowing teams that race on the Ohio and Muskingum Rivers, would be good exercise to strengthen his neck. He tried it, and that, according to his family, was when he fell in love with the beauty of the river and the thrill of boating. Soon, if he wasn't rowing, he was in his family's pleasure boat zipping up and down the confluence of the two rivers, learning the vagaries of river boating, absorbing the legends and the lore of the water.

He became acquainted with towboat captains who pushed the huge barges up and down the Ohio. He learned to handle a boat in all kinds of weather, in the dark and at dawn, in rain and wind.

But in his last year of college he was drafted into the U.S. Army. The Korean War was in its second year. He and his girlfriend, Peggy, decided to get married before he left for the service.

Instead of Korea, the army sent him to Fort Belvoir, Virginia, where he learned to make maps and was a topographic instructor. He lived in Washington, D.C., during his army hitch, and Peggy was able to be with him and even got a job herself, working at the Pentagon for the Department of the Navy.

After his army days were over, he and Peggy moved back to Marietta, and he finished college and obtained his degree. Then he went to work for a while in his father's contracting business. For the next twenty years he did construction work for various firms, traveling all over the country, sometimes apart from his growing family for months on end. It was that separation and his love for the water that brought, Jim, Peggy, and their sons, Jim Jr., and Jason ("J.J.") back to Marietta.

The history of the town was intertwined with the history of the river and the great sternwheelers that had once called it home. Now most were gone. Only an occasional visit from ships like the *Delta Queen,* just passing through, reminded residents and visitors of how important the sternwheelers had been to the economy of Marietta and of the adventure and charm they had provided.

Marietta was home to the Ohio River Museum. There, the *W. P. Snyder,* the last of the steam-powered sternwheelers, was open for viewing but going nowhere, docked forever. Visitors to Marietta could only occasionally see the splash of the great wheels driving sternwheelers by the levee at the river's edge.

Perhaps it was one of these great boats passing by the levee that inspired Jim Sands in 1973 to build his own sternwheeler and carry passengers once more on a regular basis from right here in Marietta.

In 1973 Sands and a partner started building a true sternwheeler excursion boat. It was to be seventy-one feet long and eighteen feet wide, with two decks and a pilothouse. It would carry ninety-eight people on a trip on the Ohio or Muskingum River. He decided to name it the *Valley Gem.* That was also the name of a nineteenth-century packet boat that had run from Zanesville, Ohio, to McConnellsville, on the Muskingum River, well into the twentieth century. (Packet boats were sternwheelers that carried both passengers and cargo.)

The new sternwheeler was an instant success. People lined up to take nostalgic rides on the craft. Within a year Sands bought out his partner and became the sole owner of the *Valley Gem.*

"Jim took a real chance making that kind of investment," recalled

Harley Noland, owner of the Levee House Restaurant and other local businesses. "Jim Sands didn't wait for people to find him, he went out and worked hard to bring tourists here."

John Briley, retired director of the famous Campus Martius Museum in Marietta, agreed: "Jim was attracting tourists long before there was any formal tourist organizations." Briley added, "He was a real River Man, rough on the outside, but with a heart of gold, who would do anything for you."

And he did whatever it took. There were afternoon cruises, moonlight cruises, discovery cruises, and autumn foliage cruises. He rented the boat out for weddings, reunions, and meetings. Even in the wintertime, through the holidays, he strung lights on the boat and, sometimes with ice coating the decks, cruised through frigid waters to bring Santa Claus to a children's party.

Perhaps his most memorable trips were the annual fall cruises up the Muskingum River, giving a new generation a chance to see what riverboat life in the 1900s was all about. They would make a passage through the Devol hand-operated locks that raised the ship above the dam and allowed it to go farther up the Muskingum, much as the original *Valley Gem* had done a century before.

Outside of Marietta, the *Valley Gem* became the unofficial symbol of the town. People all over three states recognized the little ship, and a ride on it became a "must-do" for visitors to the riverside community. Even the forty-first president of the United States, George H. W. Bush, came aboard for a ride during a campaign stop in Marietta.

Down through the years the crew of the *Valley Gem* was always small—just Captain Sands, his son Captain "Jimmy" Sands, or Captain Don Sandford, who has been described as an "honorary member" of the Sands family. In 1974, when the *Valley Gem* was first launched, Don was just a small youngster taking his first ride. He never forgot that ride and in 1985 started working on the ship, eventually working his way up to captain. One or two teenage deckhands usually rounded out the crew.

Jim had a regular narration that he would give to passengers, pointing out historic spots along the riverbanks, but he would often interrupt it with stories about the river and its occupants. He was a walking encyclopedia of facts about passing riverboats and barges; he often knew the names of not only the captains but also members of the crew.

He became a one-man welcoming committee for the town, telling his passengers of the many things to see and do in the valley, providing tips on restaurants and places to stay and, along with river lore, passing on the history of his adopted town.

For visiting reporters he became an unofficial spokesman for the riverfront community. He could round up public officials with just one call from his ship-to-shore telephone; he knew just about everyone in his community, and they knew him.

He had long seen the need for a larger boat to accommodate the increasing number of tourists to his little town. With the help of a friend, Ivan Arnold, a master welder, and recent college graduate Don Sandford, he started work in a field along the Ohio River, just outside of town, on a new ship that would be a much larger, more modern version of the *Valley Gem*. In 1989 the *Valley Gem II* was launched. It was a labor of love, specially designed for the low bridges of the river. Though bigger and longer than the original, the new *Valley Gem* could still fit through the historic locks on the Muskingum River. With Jim Sands behind the wheel in the pilothouse, it seemed as if he and the ship became one.

But in 1990 tragedy struck the Sands family. Jim's son, 32-year-old Jimmy Sands, passed away after a long battle with cancer. Jim had lost more than his oldest son; he had lost his "right arm," the man he planned to hand over the wheel of the *Valley Gem* to when he retired.

Still grieving, Jim and Peggy carried on, although the pilothouse on the new *Valley Gem* seemed empty without Jimmy. To make matters worse, a bad knee was making it harder and harder for Jim to climb the stairs on the ship. Just walking back and forth from the car to the dock was agony. Yet he covered his grief and his pain the only way he knew how: with hard work. He began a new project, a barge to serve as a dock for the *Valley Gem*.

In 1992 Jim Sands had reason to boast. His youngest son, Jason, whom Jim fondly called "J.J.," became one of the youngest persons ever to obtain a river pilot's license. J.J. was just 18 years old.

"Mark Twain was an old man of twenty-four when he became a river pilot," Jim would proudly point out.

As the years passed, perhaps spurred by Sands's initiative, other sternwheelers began calling Marietta home. There was the *Becky*

Thatcher, a permanently docked riverboat that offered fine dining and a riverboat theater. Jim's friend Harley Noland, who operated the Levee House Restaurant and the local trolley service, purchased the *Claire E.* and had made her into a floating bed and breakfast. There were new museums and attractions. A Sternwheeler Festival attracted thousands to Marietta each autumn.

As the '90s wore on, Jim Sands started thinking of retirement. He had been on the river for twenty-five years, and now his youngest son, Jason, was sharing the duties of captain of the ship.

Ill health was bothering the old river man. In the spring of 1996 Jim had been diagnosed with diabetes. It was to be his last spring behind the wheel of his beloved *Valley Gem.* His health continued to deteriorate, and in 1997 he lost a leg to the disease.

A year later the man who brought back the beauty and the nostalgia of river boating for thousands of tourists passed away.

When Jimmy Sands had died in 1990, Jim had decided to honor his son by taking the *Valley Gem* out into the river and firing a volley of three shots from a small saluting cannon they carried on board.

Now, eight years later on another sad day, Captain Don Sandford stood behind the wheel of the *Valley Gem.* His crew was made up of his brother Tim, who also worked on the boat, and Jim's longtime friend Ivan Arnold. They eased the ship slowly away from its dock and made for the middle of the river. Then, facing their town, they fired three cannon volleys, the blasts echoing again and again across the river valley. It was a final goodbye and salute to Captain James E. Sands, Sr., husband, father, friend, and a true river man.

Let us probe the silent places, let us seek what luck betide us;
Let us journey to a lonely land I know.
There's a whisper on the night-wind, there's a star agleam to
guide us,
And the Wild is calling, calling . . . let us go.
—Robert Service

Today a new generation is running the *Valley Gem.* Peggy Sands has retired, and Captain Jason Sands and his wife, Kate, now operate the ship. (They met years before while she was working for a catering firm on one of the *Valley Gem*'s dinner cruises.) Captain Don Sandford (the honorary member of the Sands family) is also still there, sharing the piloting duties with Jason. A new generation of river men, and women, keeping alive some old traditions.

The Valley Gem can be found at 601 Front Street, Marietta. The mailing address is 123 Strecker Hill, Marietta, Ohio 45750, 740-373-7862; email:vgem@frognet.net

For the Birds

MARIETTA

You could say that the Thompson family of Marietta, Ohio, is "for the birds." That's a bad pun, perhaps, but these people actually make a living by just watching birds.

To be precise, it's *writing* about watching birds that has brought them fans, and, more importantly, readers, from all over the world.

Bill Thompson, Jr., and his wife, Elsa, are the folks who started the *Bird Watcher's Digest*. If not the bible of the bird-watching industry, it certainly is one of the most respected publications when it comes to identifying and caring for our feathered friends. More than eighty thousand people around the globe regularly subscribe to the little magazine about birds published in Marietta, Ohio.

Back in 1971 Bill was vice president of development at Marietta College. He and Elsa had been thinking about starting some kind of business but were undecided about just what it would be.

Elsa, who had a background in journalism, had a fascination with birds and had joined an area bird-watching group called the Betsy Birders. It was headed by a local newspaper columnist, Pat Murphy, who wrote a bird-watching column. She became a friend and mentor to the Thompsons.

"I thought I knew about birds, and I thought I was aware of the world around me," Elsa Thompson said later in a magazine article, "but once I became interested in bird-watching, I realized how much I had been missing. Here were all these wonderful creatures that I had not really noticed before."

A colleague of Bill's suggested that a magazine might make a good family business.

After doing some research, in 1978 Bill gave up his job and his benefits, the Thompsons took a mortgage on their home, and *Bird Watcher's Digest* was born.

Initially based in their home, it was modeled after the famous *Reader's Digest*, reprinting articles gleaned from a clipping service that provided them with stories from around the country.

They had apparently tapped a new market. Subscriptions trickled in, and they also began to get offers from writers with new original stories and items.

Financially, though, it was touch and go for the first few years. Giving birth to a new magazine is never easy, and Bill admits that he sometimes wondered if he had

The Thompsons of Marietta, who made a career out of bird watching.

done the right thing. He even considered giving up and going back to work at the college, but Elsa wouldn't let him. "She never gives up on anything," Bill said.

Most new publications don't survive. Only 2 percent last five years. *Bird Watcher's Digest* beat those odds, though, and saw a slow but steady increase each year, proving that their decision to start the magazine had been a wise one.

One person who received the first issue was famed naturalist, artist, photographer, and educator Roger Tory Peterson, the man who wrote one of the first field guides to birds in 1934. He liked the Thompsons' magazine and offered them not only advice but also suggestions for other items to appear in the magazine. Down through the years he contributed stories, art, and photographs to *Bird Watcher's Digest* and in 1984 began writing a regular column, "All Things Reconsidered."

By 1983 the magazine was doing well enough that the Thompsons finally were able to move the office from their home into a building they shared with a construction company. By 1986 the growth of the magazine allowed the Thompsons to purchase the building and take over the whole space.

In 1993 Bill retired and went back to his job with the college. Elsa continued with the magazine, as did their sons, William III and Andy, who started in the business as children licking stamps to help get the magazines mailed out each month. Andy took over as publisher, and Bill III became the editor.

They immediately added new ideas for spreading the word about bird watching. They now also publish two bimonthly newsletters, the *BWD Skimmer* and the *Backyard Bird News*. I met Bill III while he was conducting a bird-watching tour on board the *Valley Gem* sternwheeler cruise boat near Marietta in the late 1990s.

Bill also added to the credibility of the *Bird Watcher's Digest* when IDG Books Worldwide commissioned him to write a book in the best-selling "Dummies" series. The book *Bird Watching for Dummies* has spent years on the best-seller lists of nature books.

Nature writer and artist Julie Zickefoose, whose work has appeared in such magazines as the *New Yorker, Smithsonian*, and *Country Journal*, joined the magazine—and the family—in 1993. That was when Bill III met her while arranging for one of her paintings to be used as a cover for the *Bird Watcher's Digest*.

The little magazine that is very large in the bird-watching world continues to grow—right here in Ohio.

Cowboys in Ohio

BARNESVILLE

The Buckeye State has produced at least two world-famous movie cowboys: William Boyd from Cambridge, Ohio, who gained fame as the silver-haired cowboy Hopalong Cassidy, and Leonard Sly of Ducks Run, near Cincinnati. Folks remember him best as Roy Rogers, "King of the Cowboys."

But besides movie cowpokes, Ohio is also home to some real honest-to-gosh cowboys.

For example, the largest Texas longhorn cattle ranch east of the Mississippi River is located right here in Ohio.

It's no bull, Ohio has the largest herd of Texas Longhorns east of the Mississippi.

Truck drivers along Interstate 70 in Belmont County have nearly run off the road at the sight of steers with six-foot-long horns grazing alongside the highway. And they can't miss the sign overlooking the highway, shaped like a giant longhorn steer, that proclaims this the home of the Dickinson Cattle Company.

Darol Dickinson, the general manager of the ranch, is an authentic western cowboy. Standing about six foot two, he has been riding horses and working with cattle most of his life, except for a few years he took off to pursue another vocation, that of artist. Darol's paintings of horses are much in demand, and his original oil paintings are owned by banks and businesses in the West and some Hollywood celebrities.

So how did an artist who is also a cowboy out of the Old West end up running a cattle ranch in southeastern Ohio's coal country?

Darol says it all started in late summer 1993. His Colorado ranch had only received four inches of rain all year. The grass was about gone, and a tough winter was approaching. Hay to feed his herd was already at $100 a ton and difficult to find even at that price. That was when he met a beef farmer from Ohio by the name of Bill Farson.

Farson showed him some photos of his cattle in waist-high grass in the Appalachian foothills of Ohio. Farson also told him about reclaimed strip-mined land in Belmont County, now configured in gently rolling hills and valleys, that made almost perfect pastures for grazing cattle. He also pointed out that the area was near two major interstate highways and only a few hundred miles away from many major cities.

The following Monday morning Darol, with his wife, Linda, and sons, Joel and Kirk, arrived in Ohio to see for themselves. Darol says what they found was a place filled with creeks and streams running everywhere, grass that was thick and abundant, and, best of all, taxes that were not as high as in Colorado. In short, it was the perfect place to raise longhorn cattle.

Making the decision to move his cattle operation to Ohio was easy, but finding the land took a bit longer. They had to lease some land for the first winter operation, but by 1994 they had taken possession of what Darol calls "one of the great grass ranches of the eastern Midwest."

Now, the folks in the rural Appalachian area of Belmont County, Ohio, have done a lot of hillside farming. They've also become accustomed to the giant earthmoving equipment used in strip mining. But when a herd of fourteen hundred Texas longhorn cattle and exotic Watusi steers suddenly arrived, along with a bunch of cowboys walking around in ten-gallon hats and cowboy boots, well, to say the least, it caused a great deal of curiosity.

In Colorado, big herds of cattle are a pretty common sight, and cattle ranchers by and large are pretty hospitable folks. And for the most part the people who arrive, expected or unexpected, at their ranch are cattle buyers.

Darol said that didn't turn out to be the case at his new spread in Belmont County. "We couldn't get any work done," he complained. "We'd get people just dropping in unannounced, just wanting to see a real ranch."

Darol and his family didn't want to be inhospitable, but their business was raising longhorn steers, not entertaining tourists. "We spent a lot of time showing people around the herd, thinking they were potential customers, and they would turn out to just be some curious tourists," says Darol. Finally he decided if you can't fight 'em, join 'em.

He bought a couple of old school buses, painted them purple and white, and hired a young local girl to drive the bus and be a guide.

That solved a couple of problems: it took care of the tourists and also gave the ranch a distinctive way to escort out-of-town cattle buyers around the various pastures to see the different cattle that were for sale.

I first met Darol when I came to Belmont County to do a television story on his ranch. I dug out a ratty old straw cowboy hat from my closet and even squeezed my feet into an ancient pair of cowboy boots I had acquired years before. Darol had promised when I got there he and I would ride around the ranch and he would introduce me to the various exotic steers that he raised.

Talking with Darol over the phone, I had sort of envisioned him as "Pa Cartwright" of TV's *Ponderosa,* perhaps accompanied by Hoss and Little Joe—a Marlboro Man with leathery face, well-worn chaps, a ten-gallon hat, and a sweat-stained personality. So you can imagine my surprise when I met this tall gentleman with glasses and graying hair who looked more like a bank president and was wearing a baseball cap, not a cowboy hat. On his feet were white tennis shoes.

He asked me if I was ready to take a ride, and when I said yes, he led me not to a waiting saddled horse but to a gray Chevrolet Suburban station wagon.

"Where are your cowboy boots?" I blurted out.

"Oh, only some truck drivers and wannabe cowboys wear boots all the time," he replied. "A real cowboy wears boots when he needs to, other times he wears whatever he needs to get the job done."

Just then a man whizzed by on a four-wheel ATV.

"That's one of our cowhands heading out to round up a couple of steers," Darol offered.

"I thought cowboys rode horses," I replied.

"Depends on the terrain," Darol replied. "Here it's so hilly we have to use what we call 'Honda quarter horses' because a real horse would be exhausted at the end of the day trying to go up and down some of these hills."

But despite the baseball caps and the Hondas, this is still a working ranch; there are cattle roundups and all the other work that goes with ranching. When they move a herd of longhorn steers down Muskrat Road, the main highway through the ranch, it's an impressive sight that matches anything you have seen in the movies or on television.

By the way, besides being a cowboy and an artist Darol is also an author. In 2004 he wrote a book—*Fillet of Horn*—filled with essays about his adventures in the cattle business, where he has crossed paths with such diverse people as professional wrestler "Andre the Giant," Arnold Schwarzenegger, Colonel Oliver North, and John Wayne Bobbitt. He provided Bobbitt with a hideout from the media after Bobbitt's wife cast him into the tabloids by emasculating him one evening. While the sensational trial was going on, Bobbitt's attorneys wanted him out of the limelight and so arranged for him to spend some time working on Darol's ranch.

The Belmont County ranch is fast becoming one of the major tourist attractions of southeast Ohio.

Darol Dickinson a real-life cowboy who has brought a bit of the Old West to the Buckeye State.

Dickinson Cattle Company, 35500 Muskrat Road, Barnesville, Ohio 43713, www. texaslonghorn.com

CENTRAL OHIO

The Klems of Newark

NEWARK

Louis Klem of Newark, Ohio, just didn't seem to have any good luck.

Throughout his life he was plagued by bad fortune. His mother was killed when he was only five years old, run over by a train while walking across a rail yard in Newark.

He suffered from bad health from the time he was just a boy. When he reached adulthood he decided to go out West in search of a better climate that might help his health.

There, Lady Luck played another dirty trick on him. He met up with another Ohioan, George Armstrong Custer, who was about to go on an expedition against the Sioux Indians. Custer invited the sickly Klem to accompany the 7th Cavalry on their mission.

The rest, as they say, is history. The Sioux wiped out Custer and his entire command, including Louis Klem, during the Battle of Little Big Horn in Montana in 1876.

But how did Klem, a civilian with no military background, come to be invited by the Civil War hero George Armstrong Custer to accompany him on a mission? It might have been the fame of Louis Klem's brother, John.

John "Johnny" Klem won nationwide attention during the Civil War for his bravery. He was an 11-year-old Union drummer boy at the Battle of Shiloh, where a Confederate cannonball narrowly missed him and tore through his drum. Klem (some mistakenly spelled it "Clem") was one of the youngest soldiers in the Civil War. This was one of the last wars in which children under the age of 17

Perhaps the only known picture of Johnny Clem and his younger brother, Louis, who lost his life with General Custer.

were allowed to enlist, on both sides. Most of the little boys were classified as musicians, or drummer boys.

The drum was used to signal troops to advance or retreat because the noise carried well, even in battle. The drum was also used to set the pace on long marches.

Young John Klem saw a lot of action, from Shiloh all the way to Atlanta with Sherman. He was eventually promoted to lance sergeant on the staff of General George Thomas.

But he gained national fame during the battle of Chickamauga, in Georgia. Klem's company was in retreat, and Klem was riding on the artillery caisson. A Confederate officer spotted the tiny soldier on the cannon and demanded he surrender. Klem, then age 12, picked up a rifle and shot and killed the Confederate. Newspapers picked up the story of the plucky little boy's bravery, and soon it was spread all over the North. He became widely known as "Johnny Clem, the drummer boy of Chickamauga." He was discharged in 1864, at the ripe old age of 13.

He was later given an appointment to West Point, but, having spent most of his formative years with the army and not in school, he flunked the admissions test. President Ulysses S. Grant decided the army needed a young man with that much spunk, though, and directly appointed him a second lieutenant in 1871. Klem by that time had changed his name to John Lincoln Clem, accepting the spelling used by reporters and adding the middle name to honor Abraham Lincoln, whom he idolized.

John Klem went on to become the very last Civil War soldier still on active duty with the U.S. Army when he retired in 1915 with the rank of major general. He is buried in Arlington National Cemetery.

Many years after his death, James Rhodes, who would one day become governor of Ohio, wrote a book about Johnny Klem, called *Johnny Shiloh*. Walt Disney liked the book so much he made a movie of the story.

One final interesting note on the John Klem story. In the final days of the Civil War, Union Army bandmaster Patrick S. Gilmore wrote a patriotic song that some believe was inspired by the exploits of the little boy soldier, John Klem. You have probably heard the song. It's called "When Johnny Comes Marching Home Again."

The Real Horse Whisperer

GROVEPORT

If you love horses, you may have heard of John Rarey. If you haven't, you should.

John Rarey was born in Groveport, Ohio, near Columbus in 1827. When he was twelve years old his father bought a thoroughbred colt for a bargain price. The reason for the low price was that the young horse was a problem. No one had been able to tame the wild-acting animal. Adam Rarey, John's father, had trained many horses and felt this colt would be no challenge for him.

He took the colt into a corral, and when he tried to put a blanket over his back, the horse reared. Adam took a whip and cracked the animal across the back. The horse kicked, barely missing Adam. He struck the animal again with his whip, this time on the face, between the eyes. The horse went wild, rearing and kicking and finally toppling over, pinning Adam's legs beneath his great weight as he smashed into the corral gate.

Friends carried Adam, bleeding and with a broken leg, out of the corral toward his house. He looked back at the now trembling horse that stood snorting and trembling, ears still laid back. He gave instructions to one of the men to shoot the horse.

After they got Adam into the house and made him comfortable, one of the men picked up a gun and started for the corral to follow Adam's instructions to destroy the colt. But the corral was empty. The gate was standing open. It appeared that the animal had escaped. He ran to get some neighbors to help hunt for the horse, but when he returned the colt suddenly came trotting around the corner of the barn with a small figure riding him. It was Adam's son, John Rarey.

He asked the men not to shoot the horse, pointing out that he had been able to climb aboard and ride the colt and that, handled right, the horse was no threat to anyone. It wasn't long before the colt was following John around the barnyard and eating out of his hand.

The word spread, and neighbors brought their horses to young John Rarey to train. But no one knew how he did it. He refused to tell what his method was and insisted on being alone with the horse for a while before he would attempt to ride it. No matter how wild the animal was, after a short period in private with John Rarey, it was docile and could be handled by just about anyone.

Some suspected John of using drugs; others thought the boy was a warlock casting spells on the horses. But John refused to respond to these speculations. He was certainly taming some of the wildest horses in Ohio, though, and no one really cared just how he managed to do it.

By the time John was 20 years old, his fame as a horse trainer had spread across the country. A group of Texans challenged him to come to Texas and try to train some of their wild mustangs. It was one thing to break a farm-raised horse, but quite another to attempt to tame a wild horse from the Western range country. Cowboys had been killed by some of these horses when they attempted to subdue them or try to ride them.

Before accepting the challenge, Rarey went to Texas and spent several months studying the wild horses; then one day he announced he was ready to attempt to train them. The ranchers had arranged to have five of the meanest outlaw horses they could capture on hand for the demonstration.

They had never seen Rarey and were shocked when this thin youth showed up, not a burley horseman. Instead of chaps and a Western hat, he wore a long swallowtail coat and a starched collar and cuffs on his shirt.

Before he began he made an address to the crowd. He said, "The horse is an animal of rare intelligence and character, oftentimes superior to men in these respects." He continued, "Horses, like men, can be beaten into submission, but such methods produce no common understanding, loyalty, or respect. The horse, who is mankind's greatest servant, deserves better treatment. If I am successful here today I hope all of you will carry the message of kindness and understanding back to your ranches. I assure you, the animals in your care will richly reward your efforts."

Then he turned and walked into the barn and closed the door behind him. The crowd sat, and some ranchers began to have second thoughts about the exhibition. Fearful for the young man's life, they suggested perhaps the whole thing should be called off.

A half hour passed and then, suddenly, the barn door started to open, and John Rarey came riding out of the doorway on a huge stallion, which the ranchers thought to be an incorrigible outlaw horse, never to be ridden by a human. Rarey rode to the front of the crowd, dismounted and quietly told the horse to lie down. The horse immediately obeyed and flopped on his side. Rarey then calmly stepped up onto the horse's belly, removed his hat, and bowed to his speechless audience. He then stepped off the horse, which scrambled back to its feet. He took the halter rope and led the now docile horse over to an equally dumbstruck attendant. Rarey handed him the rope and asked him to place the animal back in the barn.

In the next several hours he repeated his performance with the other four horses. Word of his ability now spread beyond the shores of the United States. He was invited to go to England to give a demonstration of his abilities to Queen Victoria and Prince Albert.

After a successful demonstration on three of the royal couple's horses, he received a new challenge. "Cruiser" was an English thoroughbred whom some thought had gone insane. Cruiser had already killed two grooms. The horse had become so unmanageable that handlers had to use pointed sticks to drive him back from the door so they could toss his feed into his reinforced box stall. At the slightest provocation the horse would smash into the walls, kicking and screaming, and bite anyone that came near him. His owner finally had to have an iron muzzle constructed so trainers could work near the beast. And the only way they would go near him was to wait until he had so exhausted himself smashing into walls and doors that he fell to the ground. He was so hard to handle that he had not been taken out of his stall for nearly three years when John Rarey arrived.

Rarey's friends and associates knew of Cruiser's reputation and urged Rarey not to attempt to tame him, pointing out the horse was probably insane and there was nothing anyone could do with him. But Rarey had decided that this was the horse that would prove to the world that he knew what he was doing when it came to training, and he was going to do it publicly for the very first time. He was going to let everyone see just what it took to gentle the wildest of horses.

The London newspapers reported what happened next.

He brought a few ropes and some leather bands and spread them out on the floor near the entrance to the horse's stall. The door to the stall was a heavy, reinforced oak door with top and bottom halves. He walked to the stall and opened the top half and let the horse see him. The horse watched suspiciously, and when Rarey just stood there, the horse suddenly launched himself in a full charge toward the doorway. Rarey stepped back out of sight, and the horse slammed into the closed bottom portion of the door with such force that the barn almost shook.

Rarey popped into the doorway and spoke softly to Cruiser. The animal shook its head, backed away, and charged the door again. Again Rarey ducked away as the horse hit the door, but as the horse stood there shaking Rarey appeared again and this time managed to stroke the horse's neck before he could jerk away and attack again. This went on for fifteen minutes. When the horse began to tire, Rarey picked up the rope. As the horse, foaming at the mouth and breathing hard, slammed into the door again, but this time with not as much speed, Rarey managed to put a loop of the rope over his head and in seconds had him securely tied to a nearby ringbolt.

The horse, unaccustomed to being restrained thrashed, kicked, screamed, and bit at anything he could put his mouth on. This went on for twenty minutes while Rarey stood calmly at the door watching. Finally, spent, the horse collapsed onto the stable floor. In a flash Rarey was beside him, stroking his neck, talking softly to him, almost crooning, while he attached an odd assortment of straps to the horse. By the time the horse struggled to his feet, Rarey had placed a large belt around his belly with an iron ring hanging from it. Straps ran through the ring and were attached to each of Cruiser's front legs. John Rarey held the other end of the straps.

The horse started to struggle again, but Rarey pulled gently on the straps, which caused the horse's legs to buckle, and that would bring him slowly to his knees. Each time he went down, Rarey would talk softly to him and stroke his neck. For three hours this continued, until Cruiser realized that this slight man with the soft voice could put him down with the slightest motion on the two leather straps he held in his hands. This was a new kind of human. One that he must respect.

Rarey kept at it. Each time Cruiser's temper would start to flare, Rarey would speak softly to him and at the same time force him to his knees.

Finally Rarey reached up and stroked Cruiser's neck and slowly removed the iron muzzle. He pulled an apple from his pocket and offered it to the horse. For the first time Cruiser ate from a human hand. Then Rarey slipped an ordinary bridle over the horse's scarred head, picked up the reins, and led him out of the stable into the sunshine for the first time in years.

By late that afternoon Rarey had hitched Cruiser to a buggy and was driving him around London. He stopped at Buckingham Palace, and Queen Victoria came out and was able to pet the formerly untouchable horse. The Earl of Dorchester, who owned Cruiser, was so impressed by Rarey's talents that he made a gift of the horse to the Ohioan.

Rarey's fame had spread across the world by now. He toured England and France giving lessons in his method of horse training, and by the time he came back to America he was a wealthy man.

He brought Cruiser with him back to Groveport, Ohio, and built a twenty-four-room mansion called Cedarwood on his family farm. His books on horse training were adopted by the U.S. Army, and people from all over the world came to Cedarwood in Groveport to see Cruiser and meet the man who had trained him, not with violence but with a firm gentleness

Sadly, John Rarey only lived to the age of 38; in 1865 he suffered a stroke and a year later passed away. Cruiser outlived his master by ten years. However, it is said that after Rarey's death Cruiser began to develop his old habits again and by the end of his life was very difficult to handle. Rarey was buried in the Groveport Cemetery; his famous steed is reported to be buried on the banks of Blacklick Creek on the Rarey family farm.

Cruiser gained an unusual sort of immortality in the 1920s, when the Groveport high school adopted his name for its athletic teams in tribute to the horse's strength and spirit and Rarey's lesson that combining power and discipline brings success.

The verb "Rareyfy" appeared in dictionaries at the turn of the twentieth century. It was a tribute to John Rarey. It meant "to win by love, to mollify with oil of kindness, to tame a horse by kindness."

John Rarey, the original "horse whisperer."

The Curse of Leatherlips

DUBLIN

In Scioto Park in Dublin, Ohio, is an imposing monument to an American Indian who once called this part of Ohio home.

The monument is a twelve-foot-high sculpture of a Wyandot Indian chief with the unusual name of Leatherlips. That was what the early settlers called him, because it was claimed that once he made a promise, his words could not be changed. His Wyandot name was Sha-Te-Yah-Ron-Ya.

Sha-Te-Yah-Ron-Ya was an elderly chieftain who befriended the early settlers. He was described as a peaceful man of great dignity.

But it was his friendship with the early pioneers that cost him his life.

In 1810, following the battle of Tippecanoe, Tecumseh, the great Shawnee leader, is said to have felt betrayed by Leatherlips, because the old chief refused to join the call to take up arms against the white people.

In a tribal council, Tecumseh was instrumental in convincing the other leaders to sentence Leatherlips to death. The old man was not present. He was at his favorite hunting area along the Scioto River.

Tecumseh sent another Wyandot chief, Roundhead, and six Wyandot braves to carry out the execution.

They found the gray-haired Leatherlips on the banks of the river, not far from where his monument stands today. Some settlers who had heard of the Indians' plans to execute the old chief also arrived and attempted to mediate the dispute, pleading for the old chieftain's life.

Legend has it that it usually rains on the Columbus Golf Tournament because an Indian chieftain's bones were disturbed when they built the golf course.

They were rebuffed, and Leatherlips, resigned to his fate, put on his best clothing, ate his last meal, painted his face, and began to pray and sing his death song. The braves followed him as he chanted and led them to a shallow grave that had been prepared. He knelt before the grave and continued singing until, much to the surprise of the settlers, one of the Wyandot braves pulled out a tomahawk and smashed in his skull. He toppled into his grave. But he apparently wasn't dead yet. Sweat stood out on his face, and the braves called the white men to witness it, claiming that it proved the old man was guilty. With that they administered several more blows to the head until there was no life left in his body. They then hastily buried him and left the area.

Thirty years later, in 1840, the last American Indians were forced out of Ohio and resettled in Kansas.

In 1990 the imposing monument to Leatherlips was completed. Commissioned by the Dublin Arts Council, it was created by artist Ralph Helmick. Because there was much limestone in the area and the limestone cliffs along the river would have been familiar scenes to Leatherlips, it was decided to use that stone to build the monument. It became the first Art in Public Places project and received numerous awards.

Various size slabs of limestone are stacked and mortared to create the twelve-foot-tall head. The top of the head is open and creates a small enclosure where visitors can view the river as Leatherlips might have seen it. There is also a nearby amphitheater in the park, and the monument overlooks that, too.

Light and shadows give the face of the old Wyandot chief a different appearance from nearly every angle.

But there is also a mysterious side to the monument. Lynn Ischay, a photographer with the *Cleveland Plain Dealer* who formerly worked in Columbus, told me that each spring, just before the Memorial Golf Tournament in Dublin, visitors have been known to leave gifts of flowers, cigarettes, and even bottles of whiskey at the memorial to appease the spirit of Chief Leatherlips.

Apparently, some folks believe that Leatherlips put a curse on the tournament, causing rain nearly every year when it is held.

The story goes that when they were building Muirfield Village along the Scioto River, the bones of Leatherlips were disturbed; when the golf course opened, his spirit put a curse on it, especially when crowds come for the spring classic.

Reportedly, it rained on so many tournaments that one year they moved it a week ahead, and it still rained.

I checked, and the fact is that it has rained fourteen times in twenty-four years that the tournament has been held.

But, according to my former television colleague meteorologist Andre Bernier of Fox 8 TV in Cleveland, who has impressive meteorological credentials (he helped start the Weather Channel on cable TV), those numbers represent just a normal spring occurrence for Columbus. He says the odds for rain in the Columbus area during the month of May on a given day are about 50 percent. "The curse," he said, "was a no-brainer" for whoever started it. But then you know those weather guys; they only like to deal with facts.

So, maybe it's just a coincidence that it usually rains on the Columbus golf tournament, then again, maybe Leatherlips is paying back the descendants of those early settlers who pushed his tribe off their lands and out of the state.

The Leatherlips Monument can be seen at Scioto Park in Dublin, Ohio, located on State Route 257, 1-1/2 miles north of State Route 161. Admission is free.

The Floating Island

MILLERSPORT

There's an unusual island in central Ohio. Most islands tend to stay put, but this island floats.

Believed to be the only one of its kind in the world, Cranberry Bog floats in the middle of Buckeye Lake State Park near Columbus.

A great glacier covered Ohio thousands of years ago, and it created shallow lakes and swamps as it retreated north. The area that was to become Buckeye Lake was one of these, and on the edge of the lake was a swampy area mostly made up of a cranberry-sphagnum moss bog.

In 1826, with the advent of Ohio's canal system and the need for "feeder" lakes to supply water to the canal, canal builders impounded the shallow, swampy lake, diverting streams and creeks into it to create Buckeye Lake. As the water started to rise, the cranberry-sphagnum bog broke loose from the bottom and began to float. It still floats today.

The island is mostly made up of sphagnum moss, with a large number of cranberries and pitcher plants, creating a spongelike meadow. A boardwalk allows visitors to cross the floating island, which is now a state nature preserve and National Natural Landmark. It can only be reached by boat, and visitors must have a permit from the Ohio Department of Natural Resources.

ODNR experts are concerned for the future of the floating island, because as birds deposit tree seeds on the shoreline and trees begin to grow, their weight and root spread tears large sections of the island loose; the land mass is shrinking rapidly.

Jim McCormack of the ODNR Natural Areas and Preserves said that from an area of nearly 50 acres 150 years ago, the island has now shrunk to less than 11 acres, and despite their efforts to stop the erosion, it may disappear in another half century.

Buckeye Lake State Park, P.O. Box 488, 2905 Millersport, Ohio 43046, 740-467-2690, www.dnr.state.oh.us/parks/parks/buckeye.htm

The First Commercial Flight
COLUMBUS

We proud Ohioans grit our teeth when we have to admit that the Wright brothers, who were from Ohio, made their first actual motorized flight at Kitty Hawk, North Carolina. Of course we are quick to point out that the Wrights immediately returned to Ohio and really learned how to fly and control an airplane at Huffman Prairie near Dayton, and that all their major discoveries, as well as the construction of the airplane, were accomplished in the Buckeye State. But the fact remains the first flight took place somewhere other than Ohio.

Ohio boasts another important flying "first" that frequently gets overlooked. It happened in 1910.

Max Morehouse of Columbus had an idea. He wrote the Wright brothers a letter asking if an airplane could possibly carry a cargo of fabric, say a bolt of very light silk ribbon, from Dayton to Columbus, as part of a promotion for a sale at the Home Dry Goods Store in Columbus, which was owned by Morehouse.

The Wrights up until this time had been busy selling their new invention to the federal government and other governments around the world for use as military observation craft, and while they had considered that some day there might be a commercial use for the airplane, they had not really worked on the idea.

Morehouse's suggestion intrigued them. They wrote letters back and forth. Instead of just the bolt of ribbon cloth that Morehouse had originally envisioned, the Wrights suggested it might as well be something heavier to make the trip worthwhile. They suggested it could be something that might equal the weight of a large man, say about two hundred pounds.

Morehouse liked the idea, and so a box of fabric that contained a total of nearly 546 yards of material was prepared. It weighed just two hundred pounds. Inside were several pieces of R. and T. Pluvett Salome Silk. One of the bolts was rose-colored; the nine others were of various colors. The sale price at the store was to be $1.35 a yard. When the shipment arrived by air, one bolt would be cut into small pieces and sold for souvenirs while the other nine bolts were to be taken directly to the Columbus store to be sold as advertised.

The man handling the transaction for the Wright brothers, Roy Knabenshue, who usually set up air shows for the brothers, told Morehouse the cost to ship the two hundred pounds of fabric from Dayton to Columbus would be $5,000. That amounted to about $25 per pound.

Knabenshue wasn't sure how to set the amount for carrying freight on an airplane—it had never been done before. But because there was a lot of publicity being generated about the flight, he decided it qualified as an air show, and the Wrights' usual cost to put on a demonstration of flying was $5,000.

Just before pilot Phillip Parmalee took off, Orville Wright pasted a road map on the wing of the plane in case Parmalee got lost on his flight from Dayton to Columbus.

Max Morehouse didn't bat an eye. He approved the transaction, but he also put a few extras in the contract. Because he was paying the usual cost for an air show, he wanted the pilot, at the completion of the journey from Dayton to Columbus, to also include some aerial demonstrations and put on a sort of mini–air show, landing on the roof of the downtown department store.

While Knabenshue agreed to most of Max's requirements, he finally was able to convince Morehouse that because of the tall buildings and air currents in downtown Columbus, even the best professional "aeroplane artists" would not have the skills to safely land the plane on top of the building.

The story didn't get front-page publicity in the local papers, but it did draw considerable attention. It was announced that the flight was expected to take between one and two hours and the airplane would reach Columbus around 10 A.M. Citizens would be alerted to its arrival by the sounding of fire whistles throughout the city.

First, though, Max Morehouse had to ship the two-hundred-pound box of fabric by train from Columbus to Dayton so it could be flown back to Columbus.

Then there was the matter of a pilot. Who was going to fly the two-hundred-pound package to Columbus? Wright's three top pilots, Arch Hoxsey, Ralph Johnstone, and Walter Brookins, were all in New York doing exhibitions and might not be available.

There was also the question of what day to make the flight. November 7, 1910, was chosen, but then the promoters started changing their minds on some of the details.

Instead of morning, why not land later in the day when more people would be on hand? It was agreed to delay the flight so that the plane would arrive in Columbus near the noon lunch break to maximize the crowd possibilities. Max was predicting upwards of fifty thousand people turning out to see his box of fabric arrive by airplane.

Only a short time before, an English aviator had made front-page news by flying a tight circle around the Statue of Liberty in New York Harbor. Why couldn't the pilot do something like that on the Columbus flight? It was agreed that the pilot would do a turn around the tall smokestack at the Ohio State Penitentiary near downtown Columbus.

Max Morehouse was also busy covering his expenses. He announced that anyone who wanted to enter the landing and exhibition area to see the historic flight would have to pay one dollar, plus a quarter extra for a reserved seat. For those who wanted to watch from their automobiles, there was good parking where you could get a view of the event for just three dollars. Reportedly, he did quite well with advance sales of tickets.

But then a problem arose.

Walter Brookins, the pilot who had been chosen to make the flight, crashed and was injured during a flight in New York. The other pilots were busy, so who was going to make the Columbus run? Max Morehouse was burning up the telephone lines to Dayton. He was nervous and became even more so when it was announced that the pilot was to be a "Mr. Paimlee," whom no one had ever heard of.

Phillip O. Parmalee (the newspapers had misspelled his name) had only recently completed his pilot's training under the unfortunate Walter Brookins. He was just a rookie pilot, but there weren't that many civilians who could fly a plane in those days. Parmalee had also been flying in the New York Exhibitions and had even won a couple of minor prizes for his flying ability.

The day before the scheduled flight, Phillip Parmalee took the train to Columbus to check out the racetrack that was to be his landing field. It was a small oval track with a grandstand and just enough space for a touchdown and takeoff. He did talk the organizers into putting up some long white streamers along the edge of the field so he could better judge wind conditions when he tried to land.

The plane that was to make history was a Wright Model B, essentially the same plane that the Wrights had been selling to the military. There was no enclosure, the pilot and a passenger (in this case a box of silk fabric) sat on the leading edge of the lower wing of the biplane. The craft was powered by two Wright engines that produced only about thirty to forty horsepower and were mounted to the rear of the passenger and pilot seats so the propellers "pushed" the airplane. There really weren't any instruments; the pilot was supposed to fly low enough so he could follow landmarks like highways and railroad tracks to his destination. Besides can you imagine trying to unfold a map sitting on the edge of a wing, flying along at forty to fifty miles per hour?

November 7, 1910, dawned gray and cold.

Since Phillip Parmalee knew nothing about the landscape between Dayton and Columbus, Orville Wright found a road map and managed to tack it down on the wing where Parmalee could see it and, hopefully, figure out by taking quick glances at the map whether he was going the right direction.

It was November, and Phillip Parmalee had been flying long enough to know that at an altitude of one to two thousand feet, sitting exposed to the wind, it would be a cold ride. He bundled up. He put on three pairs of socks and three pairs of pants. Over his shirt he pulled on a sweater, a sweater vest, a heavy topcoat, and a pair of mittens. He pulled a woolen cap down over his ears. On his feet he just wore a pair of oxfords, but on top of them a pair of leather puttees helped protect his ankles and shins from the cold.

He was ready to go.

Orville Wright and his sister, Katherine, were at Huffman Prairie, the Wrights' flying field, to watch the takeoff.

"Watch the map," yelled Orville, as the plane started to taxi away, "and do your best!" he shouted as the plane lifted off the ground.

Once airborne, Phillip Parmalee immediately felt the cold air biting through his many layers of clothes. The box of fabric was securely strapped into the seat beside him. He turned the plane and put the sun on the edge of his wing. He found that he could navigate that way better than trying to read Orville's road map taped to the wing beside him. "I kept the sun-glint on the right edge of my plane's wings and flew directly east until passing Yellow Springs," he would later tell the Wrights.

By now Parmalee was shivering because of the cold as he slowly crawled higher and higher, gaining altitude, finally reaching two thousand feet. But now the cold was stinging him badly, so he banked the plane to the south to give himself more exposure to the weak winter sun. However, when he did this, he veered off course and lost the railroad tracks he was following. He turned north again until he reached London and found the railroad tracks that would take him into Columbus. As the minutes clicked by and with the motors roaring behind him, Parmalee flexed his hands, trying to get warmth back into them. Finally he started circling to expose himself to the sun for a few moments, gathering what warmth he could. Then he would turn back again until he was once more headed toward Columbus following the railroad.

Orville Wright had been so concerned something might go wrong on the flight that he sent a representative on a train with spare parts in case the pilot had to make an emergency landing. But the plane left the train far behind.

There were no problems. Shortly before noon on November 7, fire sirens, bells, and whistles started going off all over Columbus as the plane was spotted in the east heading for the city. Thousands of people rushed into the streets and onto rooftops to see this airplane that was making history.

More than three thousand people had paid a dollar each to be in the grandstand to watch Parmalee's arrival. It was just seconds before the noon hour when he circled the crowd one last time and then gently brought his plane in for a perfect landing in the center of the racetrack.

"It was a dandy trip," Parmalee was quoted as saying.

It was more than "dandy": it was the world's first airfreight shipment, and it happened in Ohio.

After Parmalee was allowed to warm up and get a bite to eat, he returned to the racetrack and proceeded to give the crowd another example of his flying prowess, even taking Max Morehouse for a ride over the downtown. Max told everyone that flying was "Great!" and that it was "no more fearful than riding a fast elevator."

Max Morehouse had had quite a day. Not only had he created a history-making event and taken a ride in a real airplane, he had also made money on the event. When all the bills were paid, in addition to gaining priceless publicity Max also cleared better than a thousand dollars, big money in 1910.

It was late afternoon when Phillip Parmalee started making plans to fly back to Dayton. But the crowd was dwindling, the light was fading, and it was getting colder. Parmalee made a command decision. He wasn't going to fly home; he was shipping the plane back to Dayton on the train. And that's how the world's first commercial flight ended.

Phillip Parmalee went on to score other aviation firsts. In 1911 he and army lieutenant Myron Crissy dropped the first live bombs from an airplane. Also in 1911 he set a new endurance record of 3 hours and 39 minutes, the longest time anyone had ever stayed up until that time.

Wilbur Wright, Phillip's friend and employer, died on May 31 of 1912. Phillip was going to miss the funeral because he was in Yakima, Washington, slated to give a flying exhibition the next day. On June 1, Phillip had just taken off and was about four minutes into his flight at an altitude of about 400 feet when a gust of wind suddenly flipped his kitelike airplane upside down. While horrified spectators watched, his craft plunged into the ground. He was killed instantly. He was just 25 years old.

Today's airfreight business, which now circles the globe daily carrying tons of material and equipment, all started with a cold ride from Dayton to Columbus on a long-ago November day, by a man named Phillip Parmalee.

Pieces of the material carried on the flight and photos of the event are in the possession of the Ohio Historical Society in Columbus, Ohio. Museum officials say they are in storage and are not on display.

Fire in the Big House

COLUMBUS

You might assume that prisons are the last place in the world anyone would want to visit. But, believe it or not, some prisons have become tourist attractions.

For example, in Mansfield the former Ohio State Reformatory attracts visitors who tour what is touted as the world's largest cellblock—also the scene of several major Hollywood movies, including *The Shawshank Redemption* and *Air Force One*.

The old Ohio State Penitentiary in Columbus might have made a good museum when it was finally abandoned in the late 1970s. It had once housed such luminaries as prisoner number 30664, whose real name was William Sidney Porter. The world remembers him better by his pen name, O. Henry. There was Confederate leader John Hunt Morgan and his raiders and, in more modern times, Dr. Sam Sheppard (the TV series *The Fugitive* was based on his case). In 1968, during a prison riot and takeover by convicts, national guardsmen and state troopers used explosives to blast holes in the roof and front wall in order to storm the prison and regain control.

But by far the worst tragedy to strike the old prison happened on April 21, 1930.

Three prisoners, never identified, were trying to break out of the pen by setting a diversionary fire with a tin pan filled with oily rags, topped with a candle, on the roof of the prison's west block. They had timed it so the candle would burn down and reach the oily rags and start a fire at about 4:30 P.M., while prisoners were out of their cells in the dining hall. The confusion would then, they hoped, allow them to escape.

Their plan hit one snag. The rags didn't burn as fast as expected, and the fire smoldered until nearly an hour later, when it finally ignited the roof at 5:30, just after hundreds of prisoners had been placed back in their cells and locked in for the night.

Prisons are usually made of steel and concrete, and under ordinary circumstances there isn't much to burn, but this was not the case in the Columbus prison.

The fire first spread to the north end of what was known as L Block and swept south through I and K blocks, where remodeling work

Flames shooting out of the cellblocks at the penitentiary could be seen in downtown Columbus.

was under way. The corridors were filled with wood framing being used to made forms for new concrete walls. The mostly green lumber gave off lots of smoke, which then spread into cellblocks G and H.

More than eight hundred men were locked in the building, which was now filled with flames and thick, acrid smoke.

Guards frantically tried to open all the cell doors, and in many cases inmates worked shoulder to shoulder with guards, going back and forth into the burning building to rescue convicts who were overcome by the smoke and flames.

When it was all over, 322 inmates died in the fire. It would be the worst fire in U.S. prison history.

Nine days after the fire, six hundred inmates were transferred to the London, Ohio, prison farm. The Ohio governor pardoned many of the prisoners who had risked their own lives to save other inmates during the fire.

At the time of the blaze, the prison held a total of more than 4,500 men crammed into a building that was over a century old and never meant to hold more than 2,000 prisoners.

The aftermath of the fire touched off a cry for prison reform. The following year the Ohio Parole Board was formed, and nearly 2,400 prisoners were eventually released.

By the 1970s a new state prison had been built in southern Ohio,

The caskets holding the remains of the convicts killed in the fire were lined up on tables in the horticultural building at the Ohio State Fairgrounds.

near Portsmouth, and a federal judge ordered the old prison closed and emptied.

The old penitentiary stood on Spring Street near downtown Columbus for many years afterward, a crumbling, rotting ghost, while some developers schemed and argued over what to do with it. Proposals to turn the place into everything from a retirement village to a shopping center were offered, but none was pursued. Finally bulldozers and a wrecking crew were called in. The walls and buildings were leveled, and the Ohio State Penitentiary became just an Ohio memory.

Today, where the pen once stood is the parking garage of the sparkling new downtown arena center.

Insulted by a Dead Man

COLUMBUS

Emil Ambos of Columbus, Ohio, loved fishing. And that's just the way he decided to be remembered: as a fisherman. In his will, Ambos, who died in March 1898, left five thousand dollars for a monument to be erected over his grave. He described just how he wanted the sculpture to look. He wrote, "It should be a life size figure of myself in fishing costume, according to a photograph taken by L. M. Baker."

The Baker photograph captured Ambos sitting on a rock, wearing his favorite fishing hat and coat. The resulting statue in Columbus's Green Lawn Cemetery nearly duplicates the scene. In Ambos's right hand is a fishing pole; by his feet, a bucket, presumably filled with bait. A broken rope dangles from his left hand, where once hung a stringer filled with bronze fish. (The fish are gone, stolen by vandals many years ago.)

Emil Ambos had inherited much wealth, but he was also known as a man who gave much to charity. And he had many friends (especially fishing buddies). Accordingly, his seventeen-page last will and testament contained a few unusual provisions.

Take item number 13 for instance. Ambos left a thousand dollars in an account and ordered his executor to have a party: "As soon as interest to the amount of two hundred dollars shall have accrued and have been paid in, he shall use and expend the same in giving a memorial fish supper to such of my friends as shall be here, together with other genuine lovers of legitimate angling as in his judgment will know how to appreciate the occasion."

The will also provided that another fish supper should be held when the funds accumulated another two hundred dollars in interest, and after that dinner the original thousand dollars should be donated to the Franklin County Children's Home.

History notes that the dinners were indeed held, one in January 1905, almost seven years after Ambos death; the other in 1908. At the conclusion of the second supper, a check for one thousand dollars was presented to the children's home.

But one clause in his will led to a bizarre turn of events. Ambos prob-

Even in death, Columbus businessman Emil Ambos was not a man to be argued with.

ably thought it was just a routine bequest. He had a farm about ten miles southeast of Columbus; it was about 120 acres with a couple of lakes and a small stream running through it. An ideal place for a man who loved fishing. The lakes were always kept well stocked with fish. He called it his "Pleasure Farm." In his will he bequeathed thirty acres of the farm, including a large lake, to the city of Columbus with the stipulation that they name it Ambos Park.

But when the Columbus city council met to accept the gift in September 1898, they were not sure they wanted it.

It seems there were several problems, not the least of which was the park's location, nearly ten miles outside the city limits, making it difficult—in those horse and buggy days—for city workers to maintain the property. But the real sticking point was the fact that Ambos had also left a list of the names of people he wanted to be the trustees of the park named in his honor. Council members wanted to name their own trustees, and so the members voted to reject the gift.

Within a week some council members had second thoughts on the matter, and the gift was rescheduled for consideration. One councilman in favor of accepting the gift, who believed in spiritualism, decided he just had to know Ambos's motives for appointing his own trustees. So the councilman consulted a medium and asked her to reach Ambos in the spirit world.

Allegedly, the medium was successful, and the councilman asked if Ambos really wanted the city to name a park in his honor. The answer from the spirit of Mr. Ambos was unexpected. Ambos is reported to have told the councilman that he had changed his mind about offering the land to the city and that he now considered the city to be run by a bunch of "short skates"

When the councilman reported back to the full council the results of his conversation with the spirit of Mr. Ambos, council members were said to be "offended and outraged" at being called "short skates" by a dead man, and they voted 11 to 7 not to accept the property— probably the first time in history that the Columbus city council, or any other council for that matter, rejected legislation because of an argument with a ghost.

What happened to the property? It was sold at auction and later became a golf course and finally a private residence, which today is located just north of the Route 33 exit ramp off Interstate 70.

Arnold Schwarzenegger's Tank

GROVEPORT

What is California governor and movie actor Arnold Schwarzenegger's army tank doing in a Columbus, Ohio, suburb?

Years ago Warren Motts of Groveport, Ohio, started a small Civil War collection in his home that eventually grew into a huge, state-of-the-art military museum.

Warren is a very determined man when it comes to the Motts Military Museum.

His interest in historic military items began with a Civil War sword that he bought at a flea market and has grown from a private collection in his basement into one of Ohio's finest military museums with hundreds of exhibits.

The particular tank in question is one that actor-governor Schwarzenegger drove when he served in the Austrian army in the 1960s. It's a U.S model M-47 used by American forces during the Korean War and later by NATO soldiers. It now belongs to Schwarzenegger, who obtained it from the Austrian government. He has given Warren Motts a long-term loan of the totally restored vehicle.

Motts first spotted the tank when Schwarzenegger had it shipped to Columbus for the grand opening of a Planet Hollywood restaurant, one of a chain of which Schwarzenegger is part owner. Motts started

The tank that Arnold Schwarzenegger drove while serving in the Austrian Army in the 1960s has found a home in a museum owned by Warren Motts near Columbus, Ohio.

a letter-writing campaign to Schwarzenegger's Hollywood office, offering to give the tank a good home at his museum. He kept up the correspondence until one day Schwarzenegger's attorney showed up at the museum. He looked over the place, liked what he saw, and a short time later the tank arrived. Since then, Governor Schwarzenegger has been a fairly frequent visitor at the museum, occasionally taking a short drive in his tank around the museum grounds for old time's sake.

"He's a very personable guy," says Warren Motts, "and he sure thinks a lot of that tank. It's one of his prized possessions. We're grateful to have it here."

But the museum is not about Arnold Schwarzenegger. Wandering around the grounds you find a self-propelled howitzer from the Vietnam War, a Higgins landing craft from World War II, and an exact replica of the boyhood home of Columbus native and World War I flying ace Captain Eddie Rickenbacker. The Rickenbacker family has donated many items that will be displayed in the home.

In the museum building there is a corncob pipe once owned by General Douglas MacArthur. In another display case is the field uniform of Vietnam War General William Westmoreland. How did Motts get these items? "I just asked for them and they gave them to me," he said.

Even Iraqi badman Saddam Hussein succumbed to Motts's persistence. There is a display case with a huge Iraqi flag and two ornately framed pictures of the former Iraqi leader. "I'm no fan of his," Motts explains, "but he is a part of history."

Motts started writing Hussein right after the first Gulf War, asking for a flag or a picture to put in the museum. He heard nothing for years, but after repeated requests, just before U.S. forces toppled the Iraqi strongman, Motts got a call from the Iraqi embassy in Washington informing him that a gift from Hussein was on the way. It turned out to be the flag and two pictures.

"Sometimes you just have to keep asking," Motts said with a grin.

His board of directors includes several well-known veterans, including General Paul Tibbits, also of Columbus, who was the pilot of the *Enola Gay*, the B-29 that dropped the first atomic bomb on Hiroshima in 1945, which, some say, finally ended World War II. Another board member is Captain Harold Sawyer, one of the original Tuskegee Airmen.

But getting back to the Schwarzenegger tank, I asked Warren Motts what the California governor told him the last time he visited the museum.

Motts smiled, and in an impersonation of the California governor he said, "I'll be back."

Motts Military Museum, 5075 South Hamilton Road, Groveport, Ohio 43125, 614-836-1500, www.mottsmilitarymuseum.org; closed on Mondays.

Flight to Eternity

COLUMBUS

When Ohio was settled in the nineteenth century, the most common bird in the area was not the cardinal, which today is our official state bird, but the lowly pigeon.

We're not talking about just any pigeon; the bird in question was a passenger pigeon.

The name is misleading—they didn't ride around on other pigeons. It was derived from the French settlers, who called the birds *pigeon de passage*, meaning pigeon of passage, or migratory pigeon.

It was hard to miss the migration; it was noisy, colorful, and very, very big. It has been estimated that passenger pigeons comprised up to 40 percent of the entire bird population in North America in the nineteenth century. Estimates of their population have been as high as five billion, with a *b*. Pioneers wrote of flocks flying overhead

This is perhaps the only species that scientists know exactly when it became extinct.

a mile wide and 300 miles long, their passage darkening the skies for literally hours.

Slightly larger than a mourning dove but with a red breast, these birds were a plentiful bounty for hungry early settlers because they roosted in the lower branches of trees, where hunters could simply club them to death. Commercial hunters would bring them in by the bushel basketful, dress them, and pack them in salt brine to be sold as delicacies. They were much in demand in towns along the canals and the Ohio River.

They were so plentiful that no one ever dreamed they might some day disappear. However, constant hunting and the clearing of the land took away much of their habitat, and by the dawn of the twentieth century humans realized that the passenger pigeon was being driven toward extinction.

Several groups tried to save them. For example, the Cincinnati Zoo bought ten pairs of passenger pigeons in 1878 to start a breeding program. At first it seemed successful; several chicks were born, including one named Martha, who became a favorite at the zoo. But the passenger pigeons born in captivity were either unable or unwilling to reproduce, and soon the only pigeon still living at the Cincinnati Zoo was Martha.

For a while there was still hope: there were still wild passenger pigeons spotted once in a while. But that hope was short-lived. A bird killed by a boy in Pike County, Ohio, in 1900 was probably the last of the billions of passenger pigeons that once filled the Ohio skies. No more were ever seen in Ohio or elsewhere.

That left only Martha at the Cincinnati Zoo.

She lived on until September 1, 1914, when she passed away, the very last of her breed.

The passenger pigeon became the only species for which the exact time of extinction is recorded.

You can see two passenger pigeons (they're dead of course—stuffed and mounted) at the Ohio Historical Society in Columbus. One of them (named Buttons) is the very one killed by the boy in Pike County. Both are in the Nature of Ohio exhibit of extinct animals.

The Ohio Historical Society is at 1982 Velma Avenue, Columbus, Ohio 43211, 614-297-2300, www.ohiohistory.org

Communicating with Chimpanzees
COLUMBUS

Ohio has its very own Dr. Doolittle. Dr. Sarah "Sally" Boysen, who grew up in Sandusky, talks to animals—and she listens, too.

Boysen grew up wanting to be a veterinarian and while attending Ohio State University in 1973 became interested in chimpanzees when she took a class in psycholinguistics. She never became a veterinarian, but she did become a world leader in trying to understand chimpanzees, the closest cousins to humans.

Boysen is now an associate professor of psychology at OSU and also director of the Comparative Cognition Project at the university, and she is trying to prove that chimps are a lot smarter than most people believe them to be.

For more than twenty years Boysen has been working with about nine chimps ranging in age from four years to over forty. Each day she and her associates "talk" to the chimps via computer.

On the day I visited the compound, just north of Columbus, research assistant Stephanie Harris was working with Bob, a teenage chimp. Stephanie was in a room with a computer, and through a glass she could see into the next room, where Bob was seated at another computer with a touch-activated screen. She would talk to him through a microphone and say words like *yogurt*; and at the same time Bob's computer screen would show a large picture of a yogurt container. Then his screen would change to a series of words, among them the word *yogurt*. If he touched the correct word, he was rewarded with a grape (one of his favorite treats).

Stephanie told me that Bob could identify foods, colors, and even photographs of other chimps and some of the human attendants.

She said one of the goals is to reach a point where the chimpanzees can tell them things like what foods they prefer, the names of other chimps they would like to be with, or whether they would like to go to an exercise room.

Boysen says the goal of the project is not just to see how high the chimps can learn to count, or how many colors or objects they can recognize, but to gain some insight into how their brains work. She pointed out that in all the animal kingdom the chimpanzee is closest to humans in their DNA. She also said, "In twenty-one years we have discovered there are very few tasks that we can present to the chimps that they cannot do."

At that point our visit was interrupted by the shriek of a chimpanzee, and a small bundle of black fur came bounding through the door and leaped into the waiting arms of Dr. Boysen.

This was Emma, a four-year-old chimpanzee who has been part of the project since shortly after her birth in captivity. Emma has "adopted" Boysen as her mother and clings to her like a typical toddler. Emma pretty much has the run of the facility, and delights in teasing a couple of cats that also call the place home. Boysen says that with the help of a computer Emma is learning colors and starting to recognize some words, learning at nearly the same rate as a four-year-old human child. Emma also loves attention and constantly was reaching for our camera until we let her look through the viewfinder so that she could see herself in the video playback.

Boysen and her work have been featured on the Discovery Channel and in *National Geographic* and *Time* magazine.

The public is invited into the research center the second Sunday of each month to "meet the chimps." The once-a-month open house gives people a chance to see the progress being made in the communication project and at the same time exposes the chimps to people other than the attendants they see every day.

Ohio State University Chimpanzee Center, 6089 Godown Road, Columbus, Ohio, 614-457-9259, http://chimpcenter.osu.edu/default.htm. The open houses are the second Sunday of each month from 1 p.m. to 4 p.m.

OHIOANS ALL OVER

The Apple Man

He never held elected office. He was not a heroic general. He was not a famous author. He was just a simple man who wandered through several eastern states. And yet he gained an immortality usually reserved for presidents or princes and entered the land of legend.

His name was John Chapman, but the world knows him as Johnny Appleseed.

He was born in Leominister, Massachusetts, on September 26, 1774, and little is known about his childhood. He started a lonely journey in 1797 that led him across Pennsylvania, Ohio, Indiana, and Illinois. Where he traveled, apple orchards began to grow.

He described himself simply as "a gatherer and planter of apple seeds." But he became a mythical figure known to children the world over.

Separating the man from the myth is a bit difficult. It is a fact that he was a very religious person, belonging to the Church of the New Jerusalem, a church that was based on the teachings of Swedish scientist Emanuel Swedenborg.

The myth holds that Chapman was a kind, simple fellow who wandered across what was then the western frontier, sprinkling apple seeds here and there. He would not graft apples because he did not believe in hurting a tree by cutting the bark.

His eccentricities probably added to the legend. He did wear a cooking pot on his head. He did often prefer to walk barefoot, no matter the season. He did prefer to sleep outdoors. He was kind to animals in an era when animals were considered primarily food and clothing.

Chapman was anything but simple, though. Certainly he was astute enough to recognize where the frontier would next be settled. He seemed always to be just ahead of the settlers who claimed tracts of land where he planted orchards. With good reason: The law then said that each family that wanted to claim land in the new area had to plant fifty apple trees during their first year of homesteading. By the time settlers would arrive, orchards would already be growing, and Chapman was ready to sell the trees (at about six and a half cents each).

The apples were actually a far cry from the sweet juicy orbs that we pick today. As anyone who owns an orchard can tell you, an apple planted from a seed will probably grow to be bitter or sour. A good orchardist will grow his different types of apples by grafting, rather than planting. But in those days apples were primarily used for making cider, not eating. When it fermented, hard cider, or applejack, was the drink of choice of frontiersmen (and women, too). It was the sort of fuel that kept many frontier families going.

At one point in his life, Johnny Appleseed owned thousands of acres of land. He exchanged trees for food and clothing and other things he needed. He often extended credit to poor settlers. Along with the trees, he would also hand out religious tracts.

He was respected by both American Indians and early settlers and often was called on to help settle disputes.

There is a legend that on hearing of an Indian plan to attack the blockhouse in Mansfield, Ohio, Johnny made a midnight run through the forest to Mount Vernon, warning settlers along the way of the impending attack and bringing help to the beleaguered pioneers in Mansfield.

He eventually left Ohio and moved west, finally reaching Fort Wayne, Indiana, where he started his last orchards and nurseries. He died there on March 18, 1845. He was 74 years old.

He was relatively unknown in the rest of America until 1871, when an article about "Johnny Appleseed" was published in *Harper's Weekly,* perhaps the most widely read publication in America at that time. Johnny Appleseed became an instant American hero.

There are markers, monuments, festivals, buildings, organizations, songs, and plays honoring John Chapman today, especially along the path he followed from Massachusetts across the Midwest, ending in Indiana. And while he is usually recognized as the man who brought orchards to the Midwest, there are some other, lesser-known things that he left behind.

He had a custom of giving the wives of farmers he sold trees to some other seeds. Usually they were herbs, like dog fennel, which he believed would help cure malaria. (It didn't, and today dog fennel is considered a pest plant.) Also it is said that he gave farmer wives seeds for a lily, the familiar orange daylily (or tiger lily) that can be found growing wild along roads and highways across the Midwest.

To some people John Chapman was a lovable eccentric; to others he is a man who was centuries ahead of his time in his love of animals and the environment. But to children he is remembered only as Johnny Appleseed.

You can see a singing and dancing version of Johnny Appleseed each summer at the Johnny Appleseed Historical Drama at an outdoor theater located on State Route 603, in Mifflin, Ohio, near Mansfield, 800-642-0388.

Laddie Boy

Warren Gamaliel Harding may not be fondly remembered as one of the great presidents of the United States, but his dog was mighty popular.

Laddie Boy, an Airedale terrier, was definitely a political asset. The dog loved attention. For example, at the annual Easter egg roll on the White House lawn Laddie Boy was the hit of the day as he mixed with children, shaking hands and nuzzling up to anyone with a friendly look.

When Harding, an inveterate golfer, would practice on the White House lawn, Laddie Boy was there to chase the golf balls and retrieve them. He also would bring the evening paper to Harding each day.

The Hardings, who had no children, returned the love by making Laddie Boy a member of the family. He even had his own carved chair in the president's office, and he would sit on it during cabinet meetings. On the dog's birthday Mrs. Harding served him a birthday cake made of dog biscuits.

Journalists became so enamored with the mutt that they began

Laddie Boy was not only the favorite of President Harding, he was also a favorite of news cameramen.

to do interviews with him, asking him questions about world events and interpreting his answers by the way he cocked his ears or wagged his tail.

Newsboys across the country loved the dog so much that they contributed more than nineteen thousand pennies that were melted down into a copper statue of Laddie Boy by sculptor Bashka Paeff. The dog sat a total of fifteen times for the sculptor. The statue can be seen today in the Smithsonian Institution.

Probably no other presidential pet has been so well remembered as Laddie Boy.

In Harding's hometown of Marion, Ohio, the local kennel club commissioned artist Chris A. Plough to do a stained-glass window depicting Laddie Boy. The window, the only one of its kind, can be seen today at the Marion Historical Society's Heritage Hall (Marion's old post office building).

Heritage Hall, 169 East Church Street, Marion, Ohio 43302, 614-387-HALL.

Edison's Last Invention

Ohio lays claim to Thomas Edison as one of her most famous sons. He was born in Milan, Ohio, and spent the first seven years of his life here, before he moved to that state just north of us.

Perhaps the strangest exhibit in the Henry Ford Museum in Dearborn, Michigan, is a tiny laboratory test tube in a glass case. It purports to contain the last earthly breath of Thomas A. Edison.

Henry Ford was a great admirer of the inventor. In the last years of Edison's life he and Ford developed a close friendship. They traveled together with other American luminaries like Harvey Firestone of Columbiana, Ohio, and Luther Burbank. Even the president of the United States at the time, Ohioan Warren G. Harding, sometimes went camping with Ford and Edison.

When Ford built his Greenfield Village, a collection of unique American homes and buildings, one of the first structures he sought to move to the site was Edison's Menlo Park, New Jersey, laboratory. He restored the building to the way it was when Edison invented the electric light. In fact, Edison reenacted the famous moment for Ford in the laboratory at its reopening, and Ford ordered the chair that the great inventor sat in that day nailed to the floor in the exact spot where Edison had been sitting. It still is fixed to that spot on the floor today.

The test tube in the museum has a card with this message: "It is alleged that Henry Ford asked Thomas A. Edison's son, Charles, to collect an exhaled breath from the lungs of Ford's dying hero and friend. This test tube was found at Ford's Fair Lane mansion, along with Edison's hat and shoes, after Clara Ford's death in 1950."

So is it really Edison's last breath? I have put the question to officials at the Henry Ford Museum several times over the last twenty-five years, and I usually get the same answer: They don't know. Supposedly there is a letter in the Ford archives written by Charles Edison in 1953 in answer to a reporter's question about the legend. According to the letter, during Edison's final illness there was a rack of eight empty test tubes close to his bedside. This was not unusual, because he had a real love for chemistry and possibly had them all over the house for experiments that he might come up with. Charles Edison reportedly

Tom Edison invented the electric light, the phonograph, and motion pictures, but his last invention was an attempt to reach into another world.

said that upon his father's death he asked the attending physician, Dr. Hubert S. Howe, to seal the test tubes with paraffin. He said the doctor did as he requested, and he later gave one of the test tubes to Henry Ford.

So that's the story. Does the test tube contain Tom Edison's last gasp, or is it just a lot of stale air?

But there is an even stranger story about Edison that few people know: the story of his final invention—a device to communicate with the dead.

According to Edison's wife, Akron-born Mina Edison, the great inventor had become convinced in his last years that it might be possible to develop a machine or device that would be sensitive enough to pick up signals from the world of spirits.

This was news because Edison was considered by many to be possibly an atheist or at best an agnostic when it came to belief in organized religion and a life in the hereafter. His daughter, Madeleine Edison Sloane, told me in an interview in the 1970s that she took issue with those who called her father an atheist: "I believe he was a deist, a person who believed in God through science and reason."

It may have been that belief that prompted him to conduct what turned out to be his final experiments.

He and an associate identified as Mr. Dinwiddie had worked for many months in the last years of Edison's life on an instrument they believed would be able to pick up vibrations from the human spirit. They kept fine-tuning the device, but it was never completed.

Mina Edison said her husband felt that, since he had solved some of the most impenetrable scientific problems of the world, his next world to conquer would be the world of the spirits of the dead. Edison and Dinwiddie made a solemn promise to each other: whoever died first would do everything possible to send a message to the survivor. Dinwiddie died first, and Edison sadly admitted that, try as he might, he never received anything that he could remotely call a message from Dinwiddie.

Despite his failure he told a friend he thought the possibility of communicating with the dead was still a "fifty-fifty proposition."

Then in October 1931 Edison suffered his final illness. As he lay dying he promised his wife, "If there is a way for me to come back and talk to you, I will come."

Two years after his death Mrs. Edison was asked if her husband had kept his promise.

She admitted she had heard nothing. But she added this thought: "I don't believe his mind is dead. I believe it will go on and on, into higher spheres of service in another world."

Some of Edison's early inventions are on display at the Thomas Edison Birthplace, 9 Edison Drive, Milan, Ohio, 419-499-2135, and at the Henry Ford Museum, 20900 Oakwood Boulevard, Dearborn, Michigan 48124-4088, 313-982-0088 or 800-835-5237, www.hfmgv.org

General Custer's Deadly Hobby

Ohio is always proud of its native-born sons and daughters who have made their mark in the world. But George Armstrong Custer, born in New Rumley, Ohio, has always been sort of a lightning rod for controversy. Perhaps part of the problem was that he moved to Michigan as a young man and made that his home.

There has always been controversy over how Custer, who graduated near the bottom of his West Point class, went from brand-new second lieutenant to brevet major general in less than three years.

However, his fearless exploits on the battlefield during the Civil War overshadowed the controversy, and he became a national hero. If he had retired then, he probably would still be remembered as a great man. But, instead of retiring, he chose to make the army his career. It was his battles with American Indians on the western frontier that again plunged him into controversy and eventually resulted in his death.

But did you know that if George Armstrong Custer had not lost his life in the Battle of Little Big Horn, there is a good chance his hobby would have killed him?

That's just one of the things you can learn in a visit to the Custer Exhibit at the Monroe County Historical Museum just fifteen minutes north of Toledo, Ohio, in Monroe, Michigan.

Custer, it seems, had taken up the hobby of taxidermy. (He loved to hunt animals as well as Indians.) The problem is that the hobby then required large amounts of arsenic to prepare the specimens for mounting, and it took quite a while before taxidermists finally realized why people in their profession were dying so young.

According to the former director of the Monroe County Historical Museum, Matthew Switlik, by the time of the Little Big Horn battle clumps of General Custer's hair were falling out, and he was showing other signs of arsenic poisoning. Had he survived the battle, the chances are pretty good that in any event he would have died in a short time.

Also, General Custer actually wasn't a general when he died. He was a lieutenant colonel. During the Civil War Custer was promoted to *Brevet* Major General, but that was a temporary title for his bravery in battle. When peace came he was returned to the rank of lieutenant colonel.

However, this fact is not reflected in the statue of Custer that stands in downtown Monroe today. Custer's wife, Elizabeth, was still alive at the turn of the twentieth century when it was decided to erect a statue to honor Custer in Monroe. Elizabeth, or Libby, as she was called, was asked to approve the model of the statue to be built. It showed Custer in his last year as a lieutenant colonel astride a horse, with two of the horse's hooves off the ground. Tradition has it that those equestrian statues with two hooves up signify that the rider died in battle. Mrs. Custer did not approve. First, the statue depicted her late husband wearing a type of uniform jacket that he had rarely worn in life. It was her suggestion that they also show Custer not as a lieutenant colonel but as a major general leading the charge during the Civil War. That is the statue you see today near downtown Monroe. The horse is standing with all four feet on the ground, denoting that Custer survived the battle—that one, at least.

The statue also played a role in Mrs. Custer breaking all her ties with the town of Monroe. While she was very happy with the re-designed statue, a dozen years later the city fathers decided to move the statue from its promi-nent location downtown to a new park they had just developed on the site of a former city landfill. While many today say the park was a perfectly nice location for the statue, Mrs. Custer was out-raged, feeling they had placed her husband's likeness in a dump. She never again set foot in Mon-roe, Michigan. Ironically, during a spate of urban renewal in the middle of the twentieth century, the statue was moved once again, to a spot near its original location downtown.

If the Indians had not killed Custer at the battle of the Little Big Horn, it's possible that he would have soon died because of his hobby.

Probably the largest display of Custer memorabilia outside of the Smithsonian is located in Monroe. The Custer family is still asso-ciated with the town and has donated many of George Armstrong Custer's possessions to the community (that is, what is left of the Custer family: five members of the family, including Custer, his two brothers, a brother-in-law, and his nephew, perished in the Battle of Little Big Horn. Only one brother, Nevin Custer, remained in Mon-roe to carry on the name).

Ironically, the museum stands on the site of the former home of Custer and his wife. The house was moved in 1910 to make room for the new building, which was first used as a U.S. post office and later became the county museum and once again home to the possessions of George and Libby Custer.

Custer Statue and Birthplace Site, New Rumley, Ohio (no phone).

The Custer family collection can be seen at the Monroe County Historical Mu-seum, 126 South Monroe Street, Monroe, Michigan, 734-240-7780.

Was Ohio Bombed by Japan in World War II?

I was just six years old when World War II started in 1941, yet I re-member clearly the fear I felt on our farm in northern Ohio when I heard the first air-raid sirens go off in 1942.

It was just a drill, but throughout our rural neighborhood the lights winked out, and we poured outside the farmhouse to gaze at the star-studded skies searching for Nazi or Japanese bombers that we really expected to see winging over our cornfields.

Of course at that time I wasn't aware that neither the Japanese nor the Germans had the technology to build an aircraft that could fly over an ocean and hundreds of miles inland to attack our cornfields.

As the war years dragged on, we became less concerned with the periodic air-raid drills that were staged locally and more concerned with the comings and goings of relatives who were in the various armed services. By 1944, when we heard air-raid sirens screaming in the night we usually just ignored them. If we still had local air-raid wardens policing our area for neighbors ignoring the lights-out rule, we never saw them. For the most part, life went on as usual, lights blazing away.

By late 1944, with American forces on the offensive around the world, I felt pretty safe in my rural Ohio community. The last thing I would have expected was a bombing attack on Ohio or on the United States.

What we didn't know was that in 1944 America *was* bombed, from the air, by the Japanese. And it happened not once, but many times.

On April 18, 1942, Lieutenant Colonel Jimmy Doolittle led a raid on Japan, bombing downtown Tokyo in retaliation for the Japanese sneak attack on Pearl Harbor on December 7, 1941.

The Japanese, in turn, wanted to retaliate by bombing U.S. cities on the mainland. But how? The plan they devised has been called, by some, one of the more diabolical schemes of the war; others have labeled it "the dumbest act of World War II."

In 1944 Japan launched a series of balloon bombs. The hydro-gen-filled paper balloons, carrying a fifteen-kilogram antipersonnel bomb and two incendiary devices, would ride the jet stream across the Pacific Ocean and, through the use of a complicated timing mechanism, deploy the bombs and incendiary devices over cities and forests of the United States.

On November 3, 1944, they released the first of what would be a total of more than nine thousand such balloon bombs. Then they waited to see what happened.

The balloons were known as FU-GO, because of the Japanese numbers and letters on the side. They were about thirty feet in diameter, made of a laminated mulberry paper and filled with hydrogen. Beneath each balloon was a small gondola that carried the bombs and incendiary devices and a mechanism to control the cruising altitude and release of the weapons.

The first balloon bomb to reach the United States was discovered on December 6, 1944, in a wilderness area near Thermopolis, Wyoming. It did no damage, but the news media reported the finding, thus informing the Japanese, who were monitoring U.S. news reports, that their test had succeeded. The U.S. government also realized the potential of this new Japanese weapon and urged the news media to not report it further. Because it was now labeled top secret, the media went along and printed no more stories about the balloon bombs.

In the next few months the Japanese released 9,300 of the explosive balloons into the jet stream headed for the United States, hoping the bombs would create chaos in U.S. cities and perhaps start forest fires in the Midwest, which would force troops to be taken from the front lines to fight fires. But aside from the news about the Wyoming sighting, there was not one word in the media after that about the bombs. The Japanese were dumbfounded. Maybe the one balloon that reached the United States was a fluke; perhaps the rest of them were just falling harmlessly into the wide Pacific Ocean.

What the Japanese and the American public didn't know was that, according to estimates by U.S. officials, more than one thousand of the bombs had reached America, coming down not only on the west coast from Alaska to California, but also all across the country, from Arizona to Michigan. Many failed to detonate, and some were shot down by U.S. planes on patrol looking for the strange balloons.

Then on May 5, 1945, in Lakeview, Oregon, Reverend Archie Mitchell, his wife, Elsie, and their five children, all under age 13, were on a church picnic. Elsie and the kids found what appeared to be a large deflated balloon hanging from a tree. They pulled it down and called to Reverend Mitchell to see what they had discovered. As he approached, the bomb went off, killing Elsie Mitchell and the five children instantly.

Because of the deaths, government censors lifted the blackout on the balloon bombs.

Local officials across the country were outraged when the news of the bombs was finally released. And of course local citizens soon turned in hundreds of false sightings.

In Nebraska one man saw what he believed to be one of the Japanese balloon bombs floating over his city in the darkness. He fired at it several times with his deer rifle. The next morning residents awoke to find a series of bullet holes slowly draining the town's water tower.

A real concern was that the Japanese, in these final desperate days of the war, might realize that they could also use the balloons to send biological and chemical weapons against the United States. After six months, however, the Japanese, not hearing of any great destruction in the United States, had given up on the program and stopped the launches.

Of the estimated one thousand balloon bombs that probably reached North America, hundreds were never found. And even now, decades after the end of the war, they could still be dangerous.

The armed forces sent up flying patrols looking for the balloon bombs over much of the country, including Ohio, during World War II, but none was ever found here. Two were found in Michigan, one of them near Detroit.

In 1955 a balloon bomb was found by the Air Force in Alaska. Even after ten years of exposure to snow, rain, and cold, the bomb was still lethal. After being deactivated it was sent to Wright-Patterson Air Force Base in Dayton, Ohio, for examination.

The Great Chase

It was a quiet early spring afternoon, March 27, 1970. I was checking the news wire machines when I heard the Cleveland police radio monitor above the assignment desk at WJW-TV 8 suddenly come to life.

"All cars in the third district, we've got a hostage situation going on at the county jail!"

Reporter Bob Franken and I both ran toward the back door of the television station. I jumped into a news cruiser with photographer Ralph Tarsitano; Franken grabbed photographer Bob Begany and his soundman, Dale McLinn. We all sped to the Cuyahoga County Jail on East 22nd Street in downtown Cleveland.

As Franken tried to get inside the jail to see what was happening, I spotted a large gathering of police officers near a ramp to a rear entrance to the building. I headed there.

Two women, 71-year-old Louise Honour and 62-year-old Norina Dellaria, both Christian Scientists, had been in the jail holding religious services, as they had done weekly for the last half dozen years. On this day, though, things went terribly wrong.

Three inmates—James Snyder and Thomas E. Thomas, who were being held on federal charges for escape from a prison in Mississippi, and a Clevelander, David E. Carpenter, who was being held for forging an auto title—had decided to use the religious service as their means to break out of the jail.

Somehow they had obtained knives and a fake gun carved out of soap. They grabbed the two elderly women and threatened to harm them if guards did not let them out of the cellblock. They then made their way to the basement of the jail, where they ran into Sheriff Ralph Kreiger, who tried to convince them to release the women and surrender. When they refused, he offered himself as a hostage to replace the women.

The criminals said no and demanded a police car with which to escape and a shotgun. A Warrensville Heights police car had just arrived in the basement garage to deliver a prisoner for booking. Unable to negotiate with the prisoners and fearing for the women's safety, Kreiger gave in and allowed the inmates and their hostages to get into the police car. When they demanded a gun, he ordered a deputy to hand over a shotgun that had just one shell inside.

Kreiger tried to stall, claiming that he had to notify police outside that the hostages were in the stolen police car and tell them to not shoot at it as it left the jail. But the three escapees were getting nervous. They placed the women in the car and, with a shotgun held against Mrs. Dellaria's head, demanded that Kreiger open the garage door. He did, and with tires squealing the car shot out of the door and up the ramp onto 22nd street.

As the hijacked Warrensville Heights police cruiser whooshed by where I stood with reporters and policemen, no one moved for maybe ten seconds, but as the car turned the corner onto Payne Avenue, chaos erupted. Policemen and reporters were running and scrambling for cars. Sirens went off, emergency lights started flashing, police were shouting commands at each other.

I spotted Begany and McLinn near their news cruiser. I ran to them, and all three of us jumped into the car and took off in pursuit of the fleeing police car.

By this time dozens of police cars, sheriff's cruisers, and cars containing U.S. marshals had taken up the chase, which now was circling Public Square in downtown Cleveland. Apparently the escapees didn't know how to find the freeways and were caught in rush-hour traffic.

If it hadn't been for the seriousness of the situation, the chase might have been funny; it reminded one spectator of an early Mack Sennett comedy. The stolen police car went round and round Public Square with a gaggle of other police cars and news cruisers following like some giant kite tail, and puzzled citizens who were just trying to get home found themselves in the middle of a mad chase with dozens of red lights flashing and the wail of a score or more of sirens air filling the air.

Suddenly the carousel-like pattern of the chase was broken as the car carrying the prisoners and their hostages shot south on Ontario and onto the Interstate 71 ramp.

Events were going from bad to worse as the chase reached speeds of 80 and 90 miles per hour. The escapees weaved their way in and out of the homeward-bound traffic, heading south.

As we approached the Cuyahoga–Medina county line, brake lights on the cruisers ahead of us started flashing as the parade came to a sudden stop. Photographer Begany swung our news cruiser onto the berm of the road, and we joined other news cars trying to get to the front of the line to see what was going on.

A lone police car from Brunswick was sitting crossways on the two lanes of I-71, blocking the getaway car. It appeared that Sheriff Kreiger and others were trying to negotiate with the escapees and their hostages. There were a few very tense moments, then apparently the threats to harm the two women prompted the sheriff to order the Brunswick car to move off the road, and the stolen car shot away at high speed to the south.

Police and reporters scrambled back into their cars and gave chase again.

It was later learned that U.S. marshals had convinced the trio of escapees that they needed to gas up the stolen police car and arranged for them to get off at a service station at I-71 and Route 18, hoping that once the escapees got off the highway and stopped, they might again try to talk them into surrendering. The marshal paid for the gasoline but was unable to convince them to give up or release the two women hostages. Once the tank was full, the fugitives sped out of the service station and drove southbound on I-71 again.

The marshal was so frustrated that he threw his credit card at the station attendant and sped off without it, following the escaping trio of convicts.

For more than two hours the parade of police cars and news vehicles headed south on Interstate 71, the crews from the various news stations trying to jockey their cars closer to the fleeing prisoners and their hostages. At each community we would pass through more police vehicles, and more news cars would join the chase. The trail of patrol cars and news vehicles now stretched literally for miles along the freeway.

When we finally reached Columbus, there was more confusion as the escapees wandered aimlessly around the city, first on I-70 headed west, then back to the east, and finally south again on I-71.

By now it was dark, and as we sped along near the Washington Court House on I-71, the escapees, who had been keeping a constant speed of about 60 miles per hour, suddenly sped up. Speeds again surged close to 100 miles per hour, and the situation got more dangerous.

Just then, ahead of us we saw clouds of dust and car headlights spinning out of control in the median strip of the highway. It turned out to be Sheriff Kreiger. His unmarked police car had blown a front tire and spun off the highway. Fortunately it didn't roll over, and he and deputies were able to quickly change the tire and rejoin the chase.

They didn't need to hurry. The escapees, using their police radio, announced they were running low on fuel again and planned to stop at the next service station.

They weren't alone. Most of the police cars and many of the news vehicles were also getting very low on gasoline.

The parade reached an exit on I-71 at Ohio Route 38, and in the distance we could see a service station. Most of the assemblage was kept on the highway while the sheriff and other negotiators drove to the service station, made arrangements, and waved the escapees to the gas pumps.

It looked like the great chase was about to come to an end. Reporters were fuming because we were being held so far back we could not see what was happening. We learned later that while an attendant pumped gas into the stolen police car, officers approached and tried to talk with the prisoners, but they didn't want to talk. They demanded some candy bars and soft drinks, which were brought to the car, and as the attendant pulled the hose out of the gas tank, the escapees went screaming out of the gas station, tires squealing, and back onto the interstate highway.

While some police cars continued the chase, the rest of us queued up at the now unoccupied gas pumps to urge the attendant to hurry and put gasoline in our cars. The poor man, still reeling from dozens of policemen and guns descending on his service station, was demanding to know who was going to pay for the gasoline that he had just pumped into the Warrensville Heights police car. While Begany filled our car, I ran inside the station, grabbed a handful of candy bars for the three of us, and hurled some cash at the lady behind the cash register. Moments later we were back in the chase, which was now far in the distance.

Fortunately, Channel 8 photographer Cory Lash, who was alone in his news cruiser, had also joined the chase in Cleveland and had continued on. Though his tank was getting low too, he had stayed with the chase as it left the service station. I was able to communicate with him via our two-way radio and discovered that after the rapid takeoff from the service station the escapees had slowed down, almost as if they were waiting for everyone to catch up. Sure enough, a few minutes later we saw the flashing lights ahead of us, and we were able to overtake Lash and squeeze into his place in the procession while he pulled off at the next intersection to refuel.

It was nearly midnight when the gaggle of cars pulled into downtown Cincinnati, and again the escapees apparently became lost. Getting off the freeway, they darted up and down the one-way streets of downtown Cincinnati. It was at this point that we lost them.

We turned onto several of the main thoroughfares, but no luck. We had just stopped at a traffic light and were trying to decide what to do next when suddenly from behind us came the stolen Warrensville Heights police car, followed by the winking lights of police vehicles from all over Ohio. It was like being in the middle of a Keystone Kops chase. With cars dashing up and down the narrow streets, a Cincinnati police cruiser and a Cincinnati TV news vehicle both tried to take the same corner at the same time, colliding side by side. The occupants shouted at each other but just kept on going, wrinkled fenders and all.

Then there was a call over the police radio from the escapees. They were going to stop at a service station to allow the two women to go to the bathroom. They had been held hostage in the car for well over six hours. The escapees warned all the police to stay back and not approach them as they escorted the women into the restroom.

I spotted Paul Sciria of WKYC-TV in Cleveland. Sciria was a Cleveland legend because of his closeness to sources in law enforcement agencies. He always seemed to know what was going on, and police would tell him things they would not tell other reporters. As I approached I heard the police officers telling Sciria that when the women were out of the car and in the restroom, out of danger, police snipers were preparing to shoot the three escapees to stop the chase before innocent bystanders were hurt.

But as we watched, expecting shots to ring out, the women came out of the car and stood between the police and the escapees, blocking any possible shot by snipers.

The prisoners, armed with a shotgun, stayed behind the women all the way into the building. A few minutes later they emerged the same way. It was revealed later that the women, sensing the danger of the moment, had purposely put themselves between the police and the men, to protect them.

Within moments the chase was resumed as the car with the escapees and hostages careened across the I-71–I-75 bridge into Covington, Kentucky, where Kentucky state police now joined the assemblage of cars.

Over our police monitors we could hear officers in some of the cars chatting and making bets the chase would go on all the way to Florida. The pursuit was now in its seventh or eighth hour, and at that point this seemed like a real possibility.

But while Ohio authorities had been reluctant to try stopping the fleeing car while it was in motion, the Kentucky state police had other ideas.

Just as we were entering a very rural area of the interstate, near Dry Ridge, Kentucky, four Kentucky state police cars suddenly boxed in the prisoners' car. Using shotguns the troopers blew out the tires of the getaway car and forced it onto the median strip. Before the car came to a halt, Kentucky troopers surrounded the vehicle and dragged the escapees out of the car.

No one was hurt, and the women were safe. Most of the news media had missed the actual apprehension. The Kentucky state police had blocked us off, as well as most of the pursuing police cars, when they boxed in the escapees. We arrived with our cameras and microphones just as they were hustling the prisoners into a cruiser and driving them away. The women had already left the scene.

One of the longest and wildest police chases in Ohio history was finally over.

Several hours later, on our way home, we had stopped just before dawn at an all-night restaurant someplace south of Columbus. While we were eating, Sheriff Kreiger, his deputies, and the two women who had been held hostage also stopped in for breakfast.

We joined them at their table. The two women told us they were tired but physically okay. Norina Dellaria said that the three convicts had acted like "true gentlemen" during their ordeal: "I don't think they meant to hurt us. They just wanted to get away."

Louise Honour said, "During the chase, we spent most of the time in prayer."

As for the three escapees, they were taken to Lexington, Kentucky, and later tried for kidnapping and transporting a stolen vehicle across a state line. All three were found guilty and sentenced to twenty years in jail.

ACKNOWLEDGMENTS

Much appreciation to the following people who helped make this book possible:

Susan Haun of the Holmes County Commissioners Office

John Kaiser of Killbuck, Ohio

Chief of Police S. Thomas Vaughn, Millersburg, Ohio

Craag Eichman, Cleveland, Ohio

Ted Pikturna, Cleveland, Ohio

Jim Pijor, Cleveland, Ohio

Ralph Tarsitano, Cleveland, Ohio

Judi Allio, Salem Public Library

Bob Glotzhober, Ohio Historical Society

Russell P. Arledge, Ohio Historical Society

Dave Beten, Geauga County Fair

Bill and Bonnie Cutcher, Oberlin, Ohio

Bill Thompson III, Marietta, Ohio

J. J. Sands, Marietta, Ohio

Rosemary Schroeder, Cleveland, Ohio

Harald Schroeder, Germany

Thomas Price, Bowling Green, Ohio

Marvin Barr, Norwalk, Ohio

Harry Wilks, Hamilton, Ohio

Jim McCormack, ODNR

Bryan Raynor, Ava, Ohio

Dr. Sally Boysen, OSU

Jim Walker, Ironton, *Ohio Tribune*

Ann Mort, Middletown Convention and Visitor's Bureau

Margaret Albright, Rodman Public Library, Alliance, Ohio

Joseph Chevraux, Military Air Preservation Society, Akron, Ohio

Mark Boley, Holmes County Historical Society

Ernie Stadvec, Barberton, Ohio

Gary Morris, Killbuck, Ohio

Zac Morris, Millersburg, Ohio

Bob Wilkinson

Bill Wolfe

Kevin Ruic

Larry Wilson, Ohio High School Basketball Coaches Hall of Fame

Mrs. James Kline, Glenmont, Ohio

Paul J. Miller, Amish & Mennonite Heritage Center, Berlin, Ohio

Ralph S. Cooper, DVM, Pasadena, California

Gary McDowell, Adrian, Mich.

Ann Sindelar, Western Reserve Historical Society

Becky Hirn, *Delphos (Ohio) Herald*

Bob Ebbeskotte, Delphos, Ohio

Danny Fulks, Marshall University, Huntington, W. Va.

Char Lautzenheiser, Canton Classic Car Museum

Dennis Dickey, Canton Classic Car Museum

Staff, McKinley Presidential Center, Canton, Ohio

PHOTO CREDITS

Photographs by the author except: p. 4, John Kaiser; p. 7, Elyria Public Library; p. 9–13, Lorain County Historical Society; pp. 15–17, McKinley Presidential Center; p. 21, Library of Congress, Prints and Photographs Division; p. 26, Ernest Stadvec; pp. 29–30, Amish and Mennonite Heritage Center; p. 31, Library of Congress, Prints and Photographs Division; p. 44, Cleveland Public Library; p. 52, Dave Beten, Great Geauga County Fair; p. 61, Fox 8 TV; p. 67, Pete Perich; pp. 79, 83, Library of Congress, Prints and Photographs Division; p. 87, Miller Boat Line; p. 89, Ron Sherman, Miami Valley Astronomical Society; pp. 92, 93, Harald Schroeder; p. 97, Marvin Barr and Mark Saksa; p. 100 (top), Ann Mort, Middletown Convention and Visitors Bureau; (bottom), Library of Congress, Prints and Photographs Division; p. 117, Dayton Metro Library; pp. 122, 135, Library of Congress, Prints and Photographs Division; p. 139, Ohio Basketball Coaches Hall of Fame; p. 147, U.S. Navy Photos; pp. 148–49, Library of Congress, Prints and Photographs Division; p. 152, Dickinson Cattle Company; p. 155, Jim Sands family; p. 161, *Birdwatcher's Digest*; p. 168, Library of Congress, Prints and Photographs Division; p. 179, Gary McDowell; pp. 185–86, *Columbus Citizen* and *Citizen Journal* collection, Scripps-Howard Newspapers, Grandview Heights Public Library, Photohio.org; p. 188, Bonnie Zurcher; p. 190 (both), Motts Military Museum; p. 192, Mellissa Luttmann; pp. 198–203, Library of Congress, Prints and Photographs Division

INDEX